# Songs for a SERVANT CHURCH

## Hymns that encourage us

to establish justice in the face of oppression and prejudice,
to welcome and care for the poor and the outsider,
to comfort the broken-hearted, lost and grieving

**kevin mayhew**

## Acknowledgements

The publishers wish to express their gratitude to the copyright holders who have granted permission to include their material in this book.

Every effort has been made to trace the copyright holders of all the songs in this collection and we hope that no copyright has been infringed. Apology is made and pardon sought if the contrary be the case, and a correction will be made in any reprint of this book.

For additional information on the copyright holders please contact the Copyright Department at Kevin Mayhew Ltd (copyright@kevinmayhew.com).

## Important Copyright Information

We would like to remind users of this songbook that the reproduction of any song texts or music without the permission of the copyright holder is illegal. Details of all copyright holders are clearly indicated below each song.

Most of the song texts are covered by a Christian Copyright Licensing (CCL) licence. If you possess a CCL licence, it is essential that you check your instruction manual to ensure that the song you wish to use is covered.

If you are not a member of CCLI, or the song you wish to reproduce is not covered by your licence, you must contact the copyright holder direct for their permission.

Christian Copyright Licensing International (CCLI) have also now introduced a Music Reproduction Licence. Again, if you hold such a licence it is essential that you check your instruction manual to ensure that the song you wish to reproduce is covered. The reproduction of any music not covered by your licence is both illegal and immoral.

If you are interested in joining CCLI they can be contacted at the following address:

**CCLI, Chantry House, 22 Upperton Road, Eastbourne, East Sussex, BN21 1BF.**
**Tel: 01323 436100, www.ccli.co.uk**

Alternatively, a large proportion of the songs in this book are covered by the **Calamus Licence**. If you hold this licence and would like to use any of the song texts, please refer to your membership information or contact Nicholas Blackford at Calamus: nicholas@decanimusic.co.uk. Please ensure that you include these songs in your Annual Licence Quarterly Usage Report sheet, within the year covered by the licence.

If you would like to join the Calamus UK Copyright Scheme or are unsure of whether the songs that you wish to use are covered by this licence, please contact them either by telephone on **01842 819830** or by email, **nicholas@decanimusic.co.uk**. More information can be found on their website: **www.decanimusic.co.uk**

# kevin mayhew

First published in Great Britain in 2015 by Kevin Mayhew Ltd.
Buxhall, Stowmarket, Suffolk IP14 3BW
Tel: +44 (0) 1449 737978    Fax: +44 (0) 1449 737834
E-mail: info@kevinmayhew.com

## www.kevinmayhew.com

© Copyright 2015 Kevin Mayhew Ltd.

The music in this book is protected by copyright and may not be reproduced in any way for sale or private use without the consent of the copyright owner.

9 8 7 6 5 4 3 2 1 0

ISBN 978 1 84867 815 6
ISMN M 57042 291 3
Catalogue No. 1400538

Cover design: Rob Mortonson
© Images used under licence from Shutterstock Inc.
Music editor: Marian Hellen

Printed and bound in Great Britain

# Foreword

Being a servant is for many **the** mark of being a Christian. It is how Jesus saw his ministry – he came to serve not to be served. He called his disciples to follow his example in serving one another. The Church, at its best, has been known for giving service, not seeking power.

The marks of the servant are obedience and loyalty, integrity and civility. Service supports the other without dominating, does what is expected with willingness, not grudgingly.

It is significant to be a servant. But it is more significant whom you choose to serve. The serving, obedient, loyal church owes its obedience to God in whose name it serves the community. And this makes demands on the Church. To serve society while being true to God can be uncomfortable and demanding. Service of the community is not collusion with its values, it is not a cosying up to its power structures. It is a service that seeks justice where there is oppression. It seeks truth where there is prejudice. It seeks to welcome the outsider when there is a closing of ranks. It sides with the poor in a society bent on consumerism. It comforts the broken-hearted and consoles the lost and grieving. It seeks the lost.

That is what a servant church should do. Tragically, history shows us that the Church has not always managed it and sometimes not even tried.

The hymns and songs in this book speak of what the servant church believes but also reminds it of what it is called to be. Their authors are among the best known and loved of modern writers, writing from a deep personal faith and from an equally deep concern for the world, its justice and the Church's role as its servant. Some of the songs are reassuring, many of them have a challenging edge about them. In general they are intended for congregational singing but some of them may best be used by having a soloist sing the verse, with everyone joining in the refrain. In the end, how they are used will be up to those who lead worship, allowing them to speak powerfully to the hearts, minds and souls of those worshipping, expressing what it is to be a Servant Church.

**John Cox**
**Kevin Mayhew**

# 1 A crown of piercing thorns

Martin E. Leckebusch (b.1962)

From 'The Psalmes in English Metre' (1579) adapted by William Damon (1540-1591)

SOUTHWELL (DAMON) SM

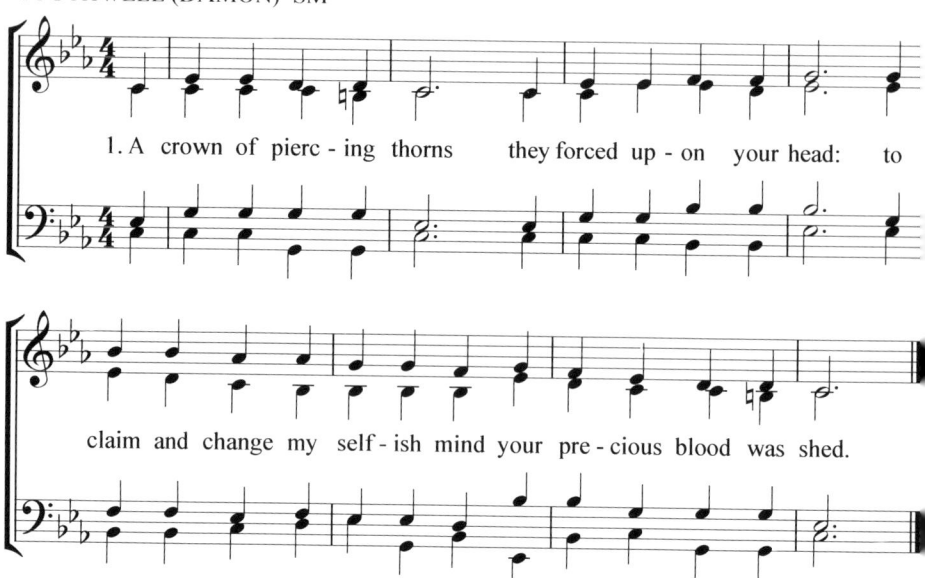

1. A crown of piercing thorns they forced upon your head: to claim and change my selfish mind your precious blood was shed.

2. The flesh upon your back
   their brutal scourging tore:
   how can I shirk another's load
   since you my burden bore?

3. Lord, how can I forget
   the nail-prints on your hands?
   Make me a servant of your grace,
   fulfilling love's demands.

4. Your feet they firmly held
   as nails were hammered through:
   my feet are free — but how can I
   not choose to follow you?

5. The spear which broke your side
   made blood and water flow;
   come, pierce my heart, that through my life
   your suff'ring love may show.

6. You took my place in death,
   your blood was freely poured:
   then let my life be spent for you,
   my Saviour and my Lord!

Text © Copyright 2000 Kevin Mayhew Ltd.
*It is illegal to photocopy music.*

# 2 All nations of the world

Edwin Le Grice (1911-1992)  
based on Psalm 100

John Darwall (1731-1789)

DARWALL'S 148TH 66 12 4 12

1. All nations of the world
be joyful in the Lord:
with willing hands your Master serve with one accord:
in ceaseless praise
with heart and voice in him rejoice through all your days.

2. Be sure the Lord is God,
creation's Source and Spring:
in him alone we live, to him our lives we bring.
From days of old
he feeds his flock and guides the wand'rers to his fold.

3. In gladness go your way:
approach his courts with song
in thankfulness to him to whom all things belong.
His name adore:
his gracious mercy, truth and love for evermore.

Text © Copyright 1992 Kevin Mayhew Ltd.  
*It is illegal to photocopy music.*

# 3 An urgent voice is calling

Nick Fawcett (b.1958)  Samuel Sebastian Wesley (1810-1876)

AURELIA 76 76 D

1. An urgent voice is calling, a voice from far away; it's crying out for justice, and yearning for that day when no one need go hungry, despair will be no more — a day at last that heralds a new start for the poor.

Text © Copyright 2006 Kevin Mayhew Ltd.
*It is illegal to photocopy music.*

2. An urgent voice is calling,
    a voice from somewhere near;
    it's crying out with longing,
    yet no one seems to hear;
    despite long years of witness,
    a multitude still search —
    forgive me, Lord, and grant now
    a new start for the Church.

3. An urgent voice is calling,
    a voice from all around;
    it's crying out in anguish,
    the grim and tragic sound
    of God's creation groaning,
    stripped bare, denied her worth —
    Lord, curb my greed, and bring now
    a new start for the earth.

4. An urgent voice is calling,
    a voice from close at hand;
    it's crying out in anger,
    campaigning for a land
    where all will be respected,
    and war will find no place —
    a world of peace and friendship,
    a new start for our race.

5. An urgent voice is calling,
    the voice of God above;
    it's crying out in sorrow,
    and urging me to love,
    for still a world lies bleeding,
    the weak go to the wall —
    Lord, help us build with others
    a new start for us all.

# 4 And can we hope

Michael Forster (b.1946)        Charles Hubert Hastings Parry (1848-1918)

JERUSALEM DLM

1. And can we hope, dare we believe, we have a share in love divine, that lifts our hearts, transforms our lives, like turning water into wine? And might we raise our vision beyond the
2. risk that love is real, daring to trust another's heart, believe the truths no words can frame, no glorious melody impart? And can we see beyond the
3. things might truly be, heavenly love among us stands; the hope for all we may become is in the joining of our hands. So let it be, let us be-

Text © Copyright 2014 Kevin Mayhew Ltd.
*It is illegal to photocopy music.*

high, and trust the best of who we are, ex-tend our
veil of dis-ap-point - ments, faults and flaws, to fix our
come a ho-ly hu - man sign of grace, to ground the

reach be-yond mor-tal grasp to catch the light of some great
vis - ion where ea-gles fail, and on-ly love e-ter-nal
world to come, here and now, and love di-vine in time and

*To next verse*

star?
soars?

*Last time*

2. And can we
3. And if these space.

# 5 At this day's end

Sean Bowman (1943-2013)        Geoffrey Nobes (b.1954)

AT THIS DAY'S END 11 10 11 10

**Slow and calm**

1. At this day's end we lay our lives before you, all that we are and think and do and say. At set of sun, as evening shadows lengthen, we turn to you, we still our hearts and

*rall. last time*

© Copyright 2014 Kevin Mayhew Ltd.
*It is illegal to photocopy music.*

2. From those we have in word or deed offended,
   from those who looked to us in their distress,
   we ask forgiveness, seek your healing power,
   give us, O Lord, some of your gentleness.

3. Father in heav'n, helped by your grace and mercy,
   let us tomorrow start our lives anew,
   and through this night, Lord, keep us far from danger,
   safe in your love, Lord, keep us close to you.

# 6 At this table we remember

Martin E. Leckebusch (b.1962)  Malcolm Archer (b.1953)

HEAVENLY SPLENDOUR 87 87

1. At this table we remember how and where our faith began:
in the pain of crucifixion suffered by the Son of Man.

2. Looking up in adoration
   faith is conscious — he is here!
   Christ is present with his people,
   his the call that draws us near.

3. Heart and mind we each examine:
   if with honesty we face
   all our doubt, our fear and failure,
   then we can receive his grace.

4. Peace we share with one another:
   as from face to face we turn
   in our brothers and our sisters
   Jesus' body we discern.

5. Bread and wine are set before us;
   as we eat, we look ahead:
   we shall dine with Christ in heaven
   where the Kingdom feast is spread.

6. Nourished by the bread of heaven,
   faith and strength and courage grow —
   so to witness, serve and suffer,
   out into the world we go.

© Copyright 1999 Kevin Mayhew Ltd.
*It is illegal to photocopy music.*

# 7 At your feet

Michael Forster (b.1946)          Alan Rees (1941-2005)

SACRUM CONVIVIUM 87 87 87

1. At your feet, great God, we offer bread, the sign of hope we share;
all the full-ness of cre-a-tion in the feast that you pre-pare.
Christ our host, in ri-sen splen-dour, gives us food be-yond com-pare.

2. Now, in humble adoration,
   drawn by grace, we offer here
   wine that speaks of liberation,
   life from death and hope from fear.
   Sharing in his cup of sorrow,
   our Redeemer we revere.

3. Here, most holy God, we offer,
   with the saints in full accord,
   hearts and gifts for your acceptance,
   broken dreams to be restored.
   All creation cries for healing;
   you alone such grace afford!

© Copyright 1992 Kevin Mayhew Ltd.
*It is illegal to photocopy music.*

# 8 B-b-b Bless this hard city

Barbara Glasson

Rod Boucher
arr. Marian Heller

**Rollicking**

*Fine* | *To continue*

*Last time*

1. B - b - b Bless this hard ci - ty with laugh - ter, crack op - en her frown with a grin. B - b - b Bless the wide ri - ver with

© Copyright 2015 Kevin Mayhew Ltd.
*It is illegal to photocopy music.*

2. B-b-b Bless the school playground with lyrics,
   let bins tap their lids to the beat.
   B-b-b Bless the wet pavements with twinkles,
   telling jokes be the news on the street.

3. B-b-b Bless the east wind with your kindness,
   the frost etch the pane with surprise.
   B-b-b Bless the fierce thunder with mercy,
   and the storm have a glint in her eye.

4. B-b-b Bless this whole city as joyful,
   the bus, bikes and train, trees and earth.
   B-b-b Bless the shut windows with moonlight,
   let the night fall be sparkled with mirth.

# 9 Be the God of all my Sundays

Martin E. Leckebusch (b.1962)

Ludwig van Beethoven (1770-1827)
arr. Christopher Tambling

ODE TO JOY 87 87 D

1. Be the God of all my Sundays, be the focus of my praise;
it is you I choose to honour on this special day of days.
God who made me, God who saved me, with your people I belong
as we come to hear you speaking and to join our hearts in song.

Text © Copyright 2010, and this music arrangement
© Copyright 1993 Kevin Mayhew Ltd.
*It is illegal to photocopy music.*

2. Be the God of all my Mondays:
   let my lifestyle make you known;
   give me courage in confession
   when for you I stand alone.
   Be my God through work and leisure,
   rest and travel, day and night;
   let me keep a clear awareness
   of a life lived in your sight.

3. Be the God I serve and worship
   day by day, throughout the week,
   God whose flawless care sustains me,
   God whose guiding word I seek.
   Be my God through ev'ry moment,
   ev'ry circumstance I face;
   God of life in its completeness,
   God of holy, daily grace.

# 10 Be the hands of Jesus

Garth Hewitt

Garth Hewitt

*Refrain*

Be the hands of Jesus, be the feet of Jesus, let the heart of Jesus be our guide. Be the hands of Jesus, be the feet of Jesus, let the

© Copyright 2012 Kevin Mayhew Ltd.
*It is illegal to photocopy music.*

heart of Jesus be our guide. 1. I was hungry, you gave me food. I was thirsty, you gave me drink. I was a stranger and you welcomed me; I was naked, and you clothed me; I was sick or in prison, and you came.

Refrain
D7
G
D
Be the hands of Je-sus, be the feet of
Bm7
F#m7
Em7
G/A
D
Je-sus, let the heart of Je-sus be our guide.
D7
G
D
Be the hands of Je-sus, be the feet of
To verse 2
Bm7
F#m7
Em7
G/A
D
Je-sus, let the heart of Je-sus be our guide.
Last time
G
G/A
2. I was treat-ed as an

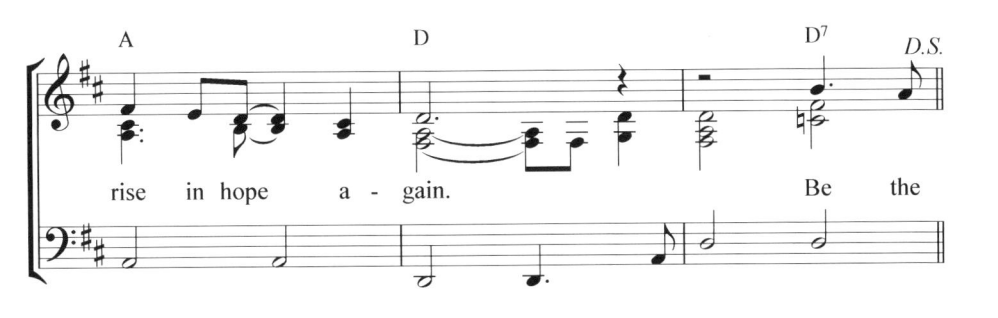

outcast. I was forgotten, I was despised. But you helped restore my dignity, you gave me back my will to live; because of you I rise in hope again. Be the

# 11 Breathe in me, Lord

Sean Bowman (1943-2013)  Geoffrey Nobes (b.1954)

BREATHE IN ME  CM

1. Breathe in me, Lord, that in-ner calm that drives a-way all fears; breathe in me, Lord, your in-ner peace that soothes a-way all

© Copyright 2014 Kevin Mayhew Ltd.
*It is illegal to photocopy music.*

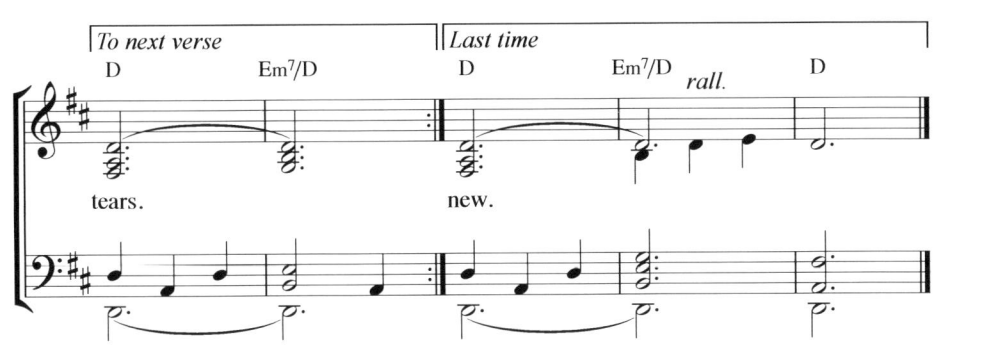

2. Breathe in me, Lord, serenity
   to face each daily test;
   breathe in me, Lord, tranquility
   that brings me nightly rest.

3. So, spirit filled with God's own peace,
   my faith is strong and true,
   and may the Holy Spirit, Lord,
   inspire my life anew.

## 12  Bring to God your new, best songs

Martin E. Leckebusch (b.1962)
based on Psalm 96

June Nixon

INGLEWOOD 74 74 D

1. Bring to God your new, best songs, all cre-a-tion; raise a hymn of gra-ti-tude for sal-va-tion; far and wide, through-out the world, sound his glo-ry;

© Copyright 2001 Kevin Mayhew Ltd.
*It is illegal to photocopy music.*

he has done a-maz-ing things — tell the sto - ry.

2. Earth and heav'ns, revere the Lord,
   your Creator;
   why make something else your god?
   He is greater!
   His are strength and majesty
   never-ending;
   ours, the privilege of praise,
   voices blending.

3. With the finest you possess
   bow before him;
   from the fullness of your heart,
   come, adore him.
   See, his beauty floods the earth —
   holy splendour!
   Yield to him in rev'rent awe —
   glad surrender!

4. All that lurks in human hearts
   he discloses;
   all that fails the test of truth,
   he opposes.
   Let the earth rejoice in hope
   of his kingdom;
   skies and oceans, trees and fields,
   join the anthem!

# 13 Called by Christ to be disciples

Martin E. Leckebusch (b.1962)          Kevin Mayhew (b.1942)

KERSEY 87 87 D

1. Called by Christ to be disciples ev-'ry day in ev-'ry place, we are not to hide as her-mits but to spread the way of grace; ci-ti-zens of heaven's king-dom, though this world is where we live,

Text © Copyright 2000, and Music © Copyright 2013 Kevin Mayhew Ltd.
*It is illegal to photocopy music.*

... as we serve a faithful Master, faithful service may we give. / to our King.

2. Richly varied are our pathways,
   many callings we pursue:
   may we use our gifts and talents
   always, Lord, to honour you;
   so in government or commerce,
   college, hospice, farm or home,
   whether volunteers or earning,
   may we see your kingdom come.

3. Hard decisions may confront us,
   urging us to compromise;
   still obedience is our watchword —
   Father, make us strong and wise!
   Secular is turned to sacred,
   made a precious offering,
   as our daily lives are fashioned
   in submission to our King.

# 14 Called to shed light

Nick Fawcett (b.1957)        Michael Higgins (b.1981)

COSFORD 89 98

1. Called to shed light where life is dark,
   where faith has died, re-kindling a spark;
   hope for the poor and strength for the weak,
   joy to a world where all seems bleak.

2. Called to be salt here on the earth,
   giving to all a sense of their worth;
   seeing the best though knowing the worst,
   putting self last, our neighbour first.

3. Called to show love in all we do,
   making the words of Jesus ring true;
   dying to self that others may live,
   eager to serve, and glad to give.

4. Called to bring joy where there are tears,
   courage and strength to overcome fears,
   purpose to lives destroyed by despair,
   comfort to hearts oppressed by care.

5. Called to make peace where there is war,
   healing of wounds still weeping and raw;
   cancelling debt and wiping the slate,
   bringing at last an end to hate.

6. Called to share life with all we meet,
   until, O Lord, your will is complete.
   Open our eyes and help us to see
   this is the Church we ought to be.

© Copyright 2000 Kevin Mayhew Ltd.
*It is illegal to photocopy music.*

# 15 Christ, here we are! *God of The Second Chance*

Lucy Berry (b.1957)           From 'Musikalisches Handbuch' (1690)

WINCHESTER NEW LM

1. Christ, here we are! We're side by side, and
wish to sing and laugh and dance. We pray that out of
our mistakes you will create our second chance.

2. Christ, heal us! open up our eyes;
unblock our minds; unstop our ears.
Restore us through your love and blood,
birth us to liveliness, from tears.

3. Burning and bleak, the wilderness
scorches our buds and chars our roots.
Pour down your loving, living rain,
to bud and blossom and bear fruit.

4. Help us to heal and laugh again;
lend us the strength to love and cope,
until we all join in the joy,
until we all share in the hope.

5. Bless you, for loving us for life.
Bless you, for your life-giving glance.
Bless you, for rolling back our stone.
Bless you, God of The Second Chance.

Text © Copyright 2014 Kevin Mayhew Ltd.
*It is illegal to photocopy music.*

*Songs for a*
SERVANT
CHURCH

# 16 Christ, my teacher

Martin E. Leckebusch (b.1962)  Geoffrey Nobes (b.1954)

CHRIST MY TEACHER 87 85

1. Christ, my teach-er, in your wis-dom great-er wealth than gold I find: bread to feed my hun-gry spi-rit, light for heart and mind.

2. Here is comfort mixed with challenge;
   here the truth is clearly heard;
   here are joys to trust and treasure
   in your ev'ry word.

3. When I struggle in confusion
   help me yield to your command,
   since by nothing but obedience
   will I understand.

4. So throughout my pilgrim journey
   let me travel at your side:
   lead me, Christ my Lord and teacher,
   Christ my friend and guide.

© Copyright 2014 Kevin Mayhew Ltd.
*It is illegal to photocopy music.*

# 17 Come, rest in the love of Jesus

Susie Hare

Susie Hare (b.1947)

**Unhurried**

Come, rest in the love of Je-sus, come, rest and re-fresh your soul; be still as his peace en-folds you, he will make you whole. Give him the things that you need not car-ry, he will bear them for you;

© Copyright 2001 Kevin Mayhew Ltd.
*It is illegal to photocopy music.*

all of your fears to him sur-ren-der, see what his love can do. Come, rest in the love of Je-sus, come, rest and re-fresh your soul; be still as his peace en-folds you, he will make you whole.

# 18 Come with newly-written anthems

Martin E. Leckebusch (b.1962)

Ludwig van Beethoven (1770-1827)
arr. Christopher Tambling

ODE TO JOY 87 87 D

1. Come with new-ly-writ-ten an-thems, craft your fin-est psalm or song;
praise the God of marv-'llous mer-cy, our de-liv-'rer, swift and strong —
he re-veals his ho-ly kind-ness so that all the world may know:
ne-ver once has he for-got-ten what he pro-mised long a-go.

Text © Copyright 1998, and this music arrangement
© Copyright 1993 Kevin Mayhew Ltd.
*It is illegal to photocopy music.*

2. Bring your hymns of celebration;
   be creative, and rejoice;
   blend as one your skilful playing,
   thankful heart and cheerful voice.
   Let the wonders of God's greatness
   be your focus as you sing;
   weaving rev'rence and excitement,
   raise the shout: the Lord is King!

3. Sing until the whole creation
   echoes to the melody,
   till the seas and hills and rivers
   join the swelling symphony:
   for he comes, and ev'ry nation
   shall receive its just reward —
   sing to greet the God of justice,
   righteous Judge and gracious Lord.

*Songs for a*
SERVANT
CHURCH

# 19 Creating God, we bring our song of praise

Jan Berry (b.1953)                                                                     Andrew Moore (b.1954)

AD LIMINA 10 10 10 10

1. Creating God, we bring our song of praise
for life and work that celebrate your ways:
the skill of hands, our living with the earth,
the joy that comes from knowing our own worth.

2. Forgiving God, we bring our cries of pain
for all that shames us in our search for gain:
the hidden wounds, the angry scars of strife,
the emptiness that saps and weakens life.

3. Redeeming God, we bring our trust in you,
our fragile hope that all may be made new:
our dreams of truth, of wealth that all may share,
of work and service rooted deep in pray'r.

4. Renewing God, we offer what shall be
a world that lives and works in harmony:
when peace and justice, once so long denied,
restore to all their dignity and pride.

© Copyright 1999 Kevin Mayhew Ltd.
*It is illegal to photocopy music.*

# 20 Creation sings!

Martin E. Leckebusch (b.1962)  
Susie Hare (b.1947)

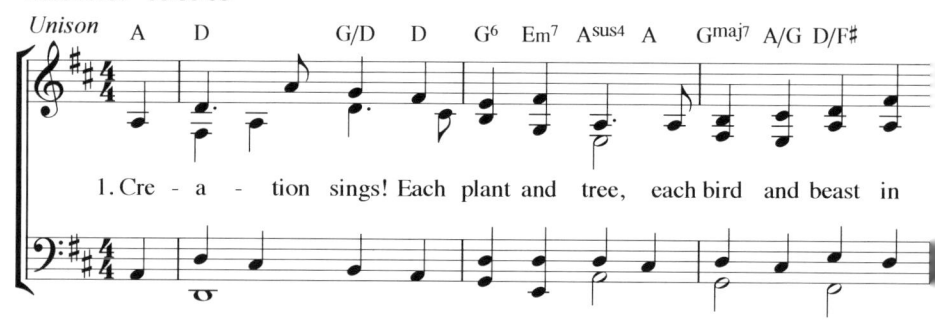

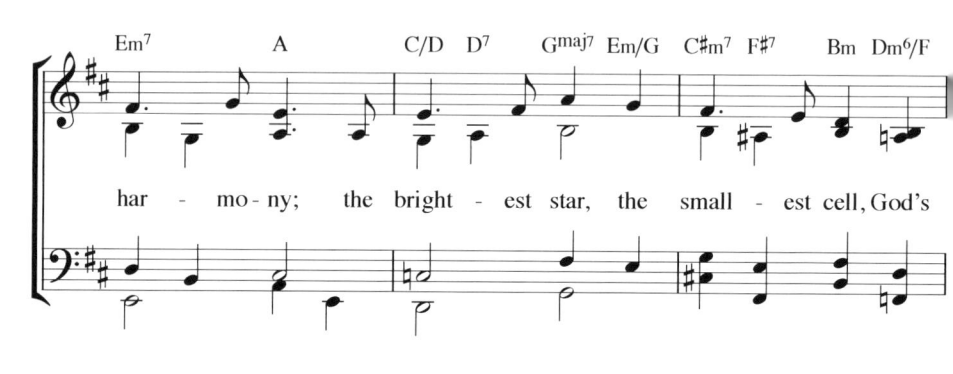

EASTROP 88 88 88

1. Cre-a-tion sings! Each plant and tree, each bird and beast in har-mo-ny; the bright-est star, the small-est cell, God's ten-der care and glo-ry tell — from o-cean depths to moun-tain peaks, in praise of God cre-

© Copyright 2001 Kevin Mayhew Ltd.  
*It is illegal to photocopy music.*

2. Creation speaks a message true,
   reminds us we are creatures, too:
   to serve as stewards is our role,
   despite our dreams of full control —
   when we disparage what God owns,
   in turmoil, all creation groans.

3. Creation groans to see the day
   which ends all bondage, all decay:
   frustrated now, it must await
   the Lord who comes to recreate
   till round the universe there rings
   the song his new creation sings!

# 21 Cry 'Freedom!'

Michael Forster (b.1946)

Traditional English melody
arr. Donald Thomson

GOD REST YOU MERRY  86 86 86 and Refrain

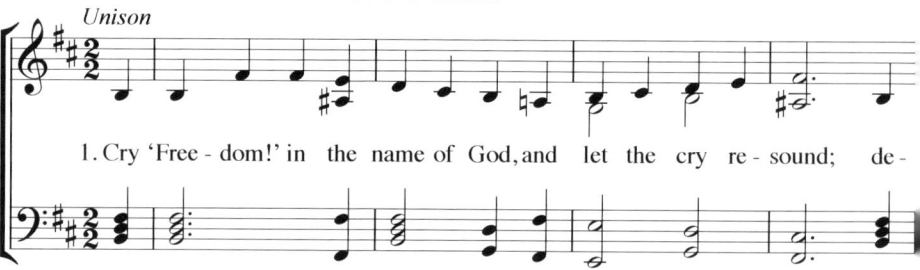

1. Cry 'Free-dom!' in the name of God, and let the cry re-sound; de-mand for all the li-ber-ty that we our-selves have found, for none of us is tru-ly free while a-ny-one is bound. Cry 'Free-dom!' cry 'Free-dom!' in God's name, in God's

Text © Copyright 1992, and this music arrangement
© Copyright 2014 Kevin Mayhew Ltd.
*It is illegal to photocopy music*

name! Cry 'Free - dom!' cry 'Free - dom!' in God's name!

2. Cry 'Freedom!' for the victims of
   the earthquake and the rain;
   where wealthy folk find shelter
   and the poor must bear the pain;
   where weapons claim resources while
   the famine strikes again.

3. Cry 'Freedom!' for the tyrant, in
   a gilded cage confined,
   who hides behind a bodyguard
   and fears the open mind;
   instead of finding freedom in
   the love of humankind.

4. Cry 'Freedom!' in the church when honest
   doubts are met with fear;
   when vacuum-packed theology
   makes questions disappear;
   when journeys end, before they start
   and mystery is clear!

5. Cry 'Freedom!' when we find ourselves
   imprisoned in our greed,
   to live in free relationship
   and meet each other's need.
   From self released for others' good
   we should be free indeed!

## 22 Don't be afraid

*Faithful Goa[...]*

Val Hawthorne, based on Psalm 91

Val Hawthorne

**Thoughtfully**

1. Don't be afraid, for God is with you. You're not alone, for God is with you. His angels will watch over you, his shadow will shelter you. Faithful and unchanging, God is with you.

© Copyright 2009 Kevin Mayhew Ltd.
*It is illegal to photocopy music.*

*Refrain*

Faith - ful God, un - chang - ing One. Stead-fast and true be-fore time be-gan. Trust in him, trust in him. Faith - ful God, un-chang-ing One.

*last time poco rit.*

2. When troubles come, yes God is with you.
   When days are bright, still God is with you.
   He knows you and will care for you,
   protects you and answers you.
   Faithful and unchanging, God is with you.

# Songs for a SERVANT CHURCH

## 23 Draw us together at the close of day

Jean Holloway (b.1939)          Edward Dearle (1806-1891)

PENITENTIA 10 10 10 10

1. Draw us together at the close of day;
here in the stillness, grant us time to pray,
space to recall experiences we share,
grateful for those who listen, hold and care.

2. Each human story, precious and unique,
lives in our actions, and the words we speak;
teach us forgiveness, not to keep a score,
help us to trust ourselves and others more.

3. Sep'rate, alone, our pain is hard to bear;
sharing our wounds, your healing touch is there.
Bound here by love of soul embracing soul,
we can be freed by love which makes us whole.

4. In your great story, Lord, give us a place;
use us to spread the wonder of your grace.
Dying to old ways, open to the new,
we seek to find a truer self in you.

5. So may we celebrate the life you give.
Told in the rich and varied ways we live;
people confined by human scale and scope,
each with a vision born of faith and hope.

Text © Copyright 2000 Kevin Mayhew Ltd.
*It is illegal to photocopy music.*

## 24 Every land in all creation

Susie Hare

Susie Hare (b.1947)

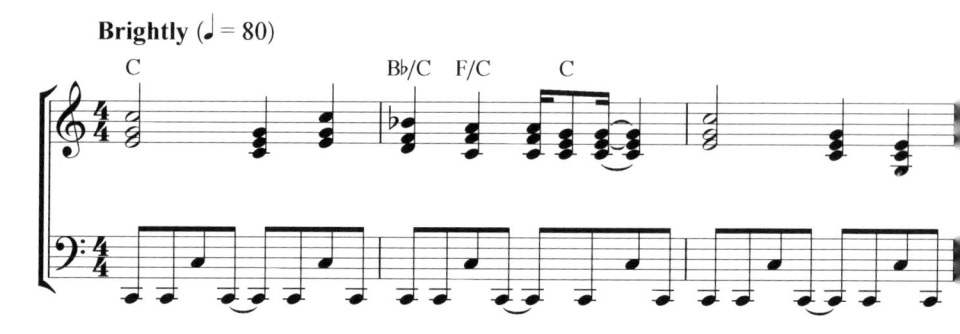

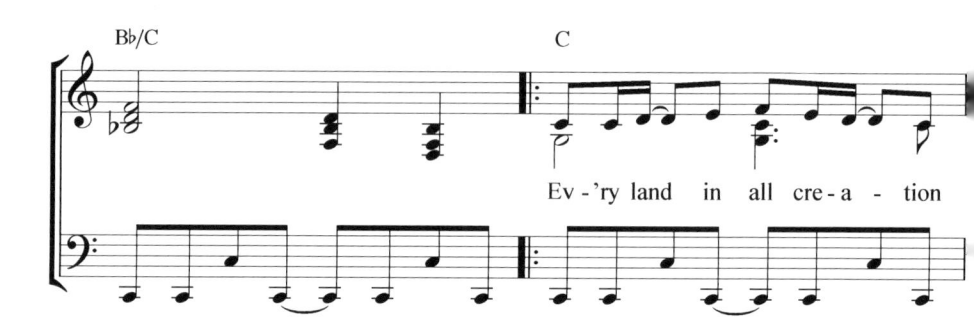

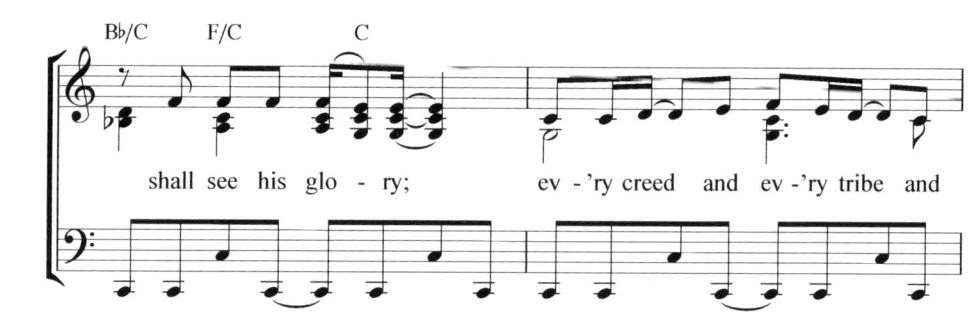

**Brightly** ($\quarter = 80$)

Ev-'ry land in all cre-a-tion shall see his glo-ry; ev-'ry creed and ev-'ry tribe and tongue. Peo-ple out of ev-'ry na-tion

© Copyright 2015 Kevin Mayhew Ltd.
*It is illegal to photocopy music.*

shall tell his story, ev-'ry knee shall bow be-fore his throne. The First, the Last, the Al-pha and O-me-ga, the one who is, who was, and is to come, will shake the earth in tri-umph o-ver sin-ful-ness. The vic-to-ry of hea-ven will be

Refrain
Gsus4 G C F
won! He shall reign for e - ver and his
G C F
king - dom shall not pass a - way. He shall reign for e - ver with - out
G C6/G G C F
end. He shall reign for e - ver and his
3rd time to Coda
G C Dm Em F G
king - dom shall not pass a - way, and we shall reign with
C B♭/C F/C C
him.

B♭/C C
Let ev - 'ry na - tion,
Bridge
B♭/C F/C C B♭/C C B♭6/C
all of cre - a - tion, join with the an-gels to sing:
C B♭/C F/C C
'Bless - ing and ho - nour, glo - ry and po - wer,
D.S. al Coda
B♭/C F6/C G(sus4) G
prai - ses to Je - sus the King!'
CODA
Am7 C/G Dm Em F G C
him, and we shall reign with him.

## 25 Extol the God of justice

Martin E. Leckebusch (b.1962)  
Henri Friedrich Hémy (1818-1888)

TURRIS DAVIDICA 76 76 D

1. Extol the God of justice with heart and soul and voice; remember all his wonders, recount them and rejoice. He stands with all who labour for what is true and right, till wickedness and falsehood are banished from his sight.

2. Extol the God of justice
   enthroned for evermore,
   a stronghold in affliction,
   a refuge to the poor:
   he hears the cries of victims
   and senses their despair;
   in faithfulness he honours
   the faith that sparks our prayer.

3. Extol the God of justice,
   however dark the day;
   the hope that calls for mercy
   will not be turned away;
   for evil shall not triumph,
   nor human sin prevail:
   the Lord is God eternal,
   whose judgements cannot fail.

Text © Copyright 2006 Kevin Mayhew Ltd.  
*It is illegal to photocopy music.*

# 26 Fearful, uncertain

Nick Fawcett (b.1957)                                                    Geoffrey Nobes (b.1954)

HALLELUJAH 9 10 10 10

1. Fearful, uncertain, troubled, confused,
   Mary, you listened, prepared to be used,
   ready to give yourself, body and soul,
   bearing the one who would make the world whole.

2. Innocent, humble, honest, sincere,
   Mary, you trusted, though much was unclear,
   willing to follow as God chose to lead,
   wanting to serve him in thought, word and deed.

3. Jubilant, grateful, spirit alight,
   Mary, you worshipped, sang out in delight:
   hope for the broken and strength for the weak,
   food for the hungry, esteem for the meek.

4. Pondering, pensive, wrapped up in thought,
   Mary, you marvelled at all God had brought,
   eagerly searching to understand more,
   hungry to fathom what else lay in store.

5. Lord born of Mary, hear us today:
   we, like your mother, would trust and obey.
   Take all we are and, in all that we do,
   help us to give ourselves wholly to you.

© Copyright 2005 Kevin Mayhew Ltd.
*It is illegal to photocopy music.*

## 27 Feast your mind on what is pure   *All the time*

Garth Hewitt                                                                  Garth Hewitt

1. Feast your mind on what is pure.
2. Fill your thoughts with what is good.
3. Blessed are the pure in heart, their

© Copyright 2012 Kevin Mayhew Ltd.
*It is illegal to photocopy music.*

| Feast | your | mind | on | what is | true. |
| Long | to | do | what | God re-quires. | |
| eyes | shall | rest | up-on his | face. | |

| Fill | your | life | with | what is |
| Let | your | life | be a | work of |
| Hun- | ger | for | the food | that |

| just, | what is right, | and let the beau-ty | of the |
| peace | and of love | and let your eyes | lin-ger |
| lasts | on and on | and dis-co-ver | the |

*1st time D.S. for v.2*
*Fine*

| Fa-ther | shine in you. |
| on-ly | on what in-spires. |
| mean-ing | of his grace. |

*Refrain*

Listen to the one who goes before you. Feed upon the bread and wine. And the peace that passes understanding will fill your heart, fill your mind, all the time.

*D.S. (last time repeat v.1)*

*Songs for a*
SERVANT
CHURCH

## 28 Finding a way

Barbara Glasson

Rod Boucher
arr. Marian Hellen

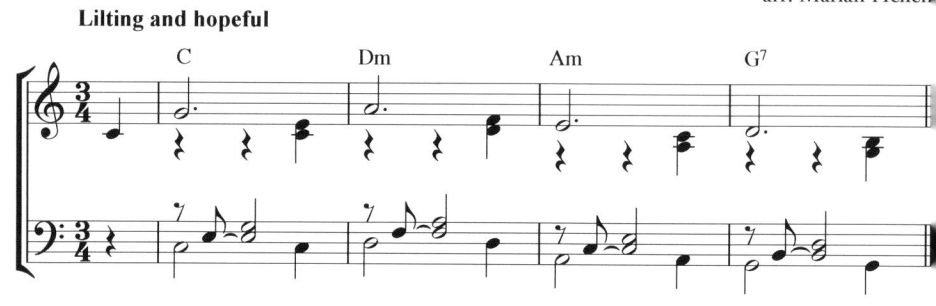

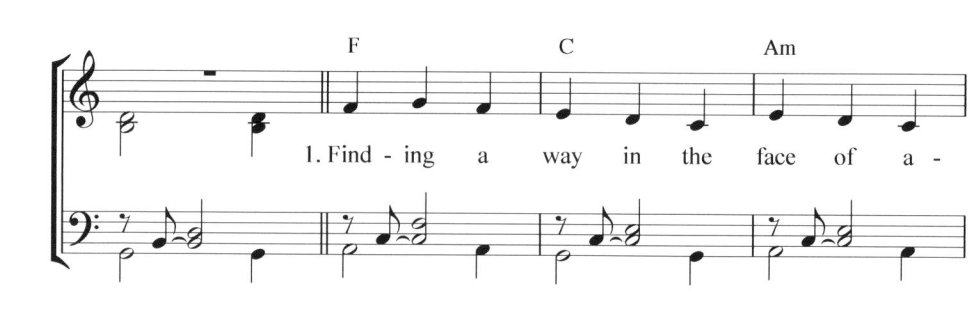

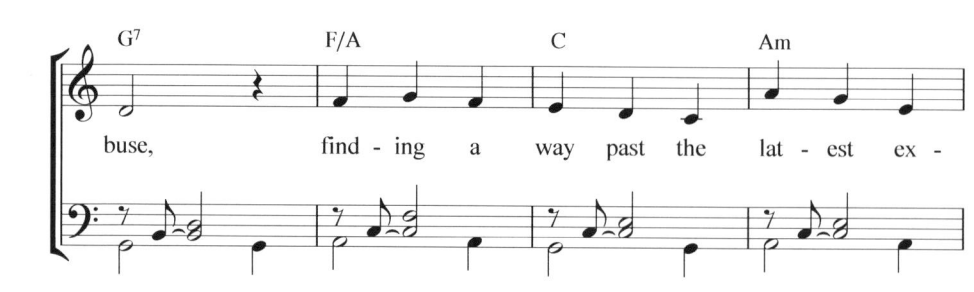

**Lilting and hopeful**

*Refrain*

Find - ing a way, just find - ing a way.

1. Find - ing a way in the face of a -

buse, find - ing a way past the lat - est ex -

© Copyright 2015 Kevin Mayhew Ltd.
*It is illegal to photocopy music.*

2. Finding a way through the words still unspoken,
   finding a way through the trust that is broken,
   finding a way to sing just before dawn.

3. Finding a way to sing into the dawning,
   finding a way we can claim a new morning,
   finding a way to the light of the sun.

4. Finding a way to the warmth of the sun,
   finding a way where the day's just begun,
   finding a way where the spirit's set free.

5. Finding a way where the spirit is free,
   finding a way to own all that is 'me',
   finding a way to live out this new day.

   *Refrain (twice)*

# Songs *for a* SERVANT CHURCH

# 29 For beauty which delights our eyes

Jean Holloway (b.1939)

Adapted from a melody in 'Tochter Sion' (1741)

ST BERNARD CM

1. For beauty which delights our eyes, for nature's rich display, for sights of wonder and surprise, we offer thanks today.

2. Creation revels in design,
   by chance are patterns made;
   the complex weave of form and line,
   the play of light and shade.

3. A palette rich with ev'ry hue
   enhances all we see;
   extravagance affirms anew
   God's generosity.

4. What God would join us in our pain,
   yet take our breath away
   by flinging rainbows through the rain
   when all the world is grey?

5. Such lavish love must come from God,
   such gifts of unearned grace;
   may we extend such love abroad
   in this and ev'ry place.

Text © Copyright 2000 Kevin Mayhew Ltd.
*It is illegal to photocopy music.*

# 30 For riches of salvation

*Give thanks*

Susie Hare

Susie Hare (b.1947)

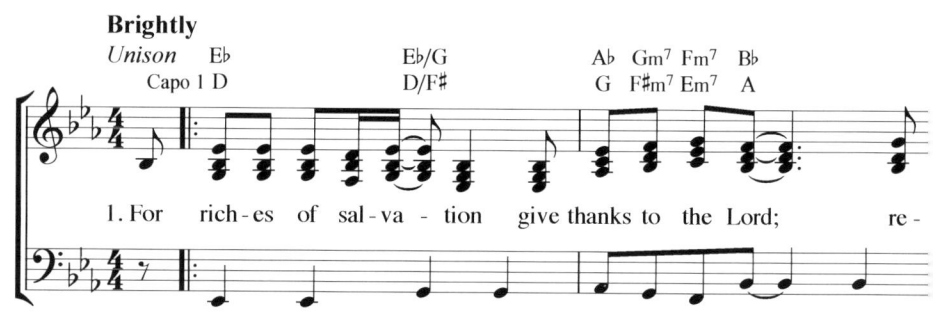

FROYLE 75 75 777 7

**Brightly**

1. For rich-es of sal-va-tion give thanks to the Lord; re-lease from con-dem-na-tion, give thanks to the Lord; for love which tru-ly frees us be-cause the Fa-ther sees us i-den-ti-fied with Je-sus — give thanks, give thanks to the Lord!

© Copyright 2001 Kevin Mayhew Ltd.
*It is illegal to photocopy music.*

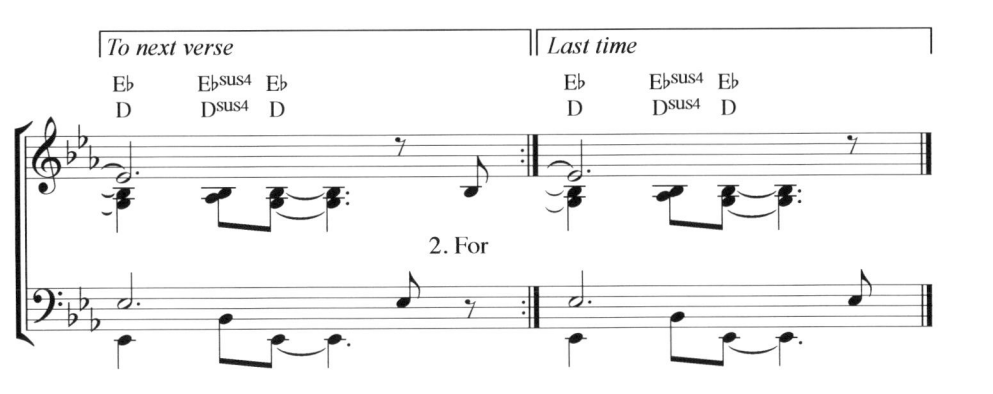

2. For courage and endurance
   give thanks to the Lord;
   the Spirit's reassurance,
   give thanks to the Lord;
   for fatherly correction,
   the call to share perfection,
   the hope of resurrection —
   give thanks, give thanks to the Lord!

3. For life in all its fullness
   give thanks to the Lord;
   for all that leads to wholeness,
   give thanks to the Lord;
   he knows our ev'ry feeling
   and speaks in grace, revealing
   his comfort and his healing —
   give thanks, give thanks to the Lord!

4. For justice with compassion
   give thanks to the Lord,
   and freedom from oppression,
   give thanks to the Lord;
   for holiness unending,
   a kingdom still extending,
   all earthly pow'r transcending —
   give thanks, give thanks to the Lord!

# 31 For those who strive for justice

Nick Fawcett (b.1957)  Frederick C. Maker (1844-1927)

ST CHRISTOPHER 76 86 86 86

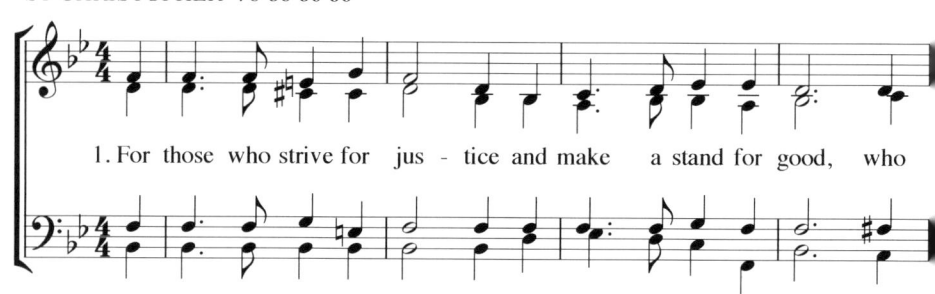

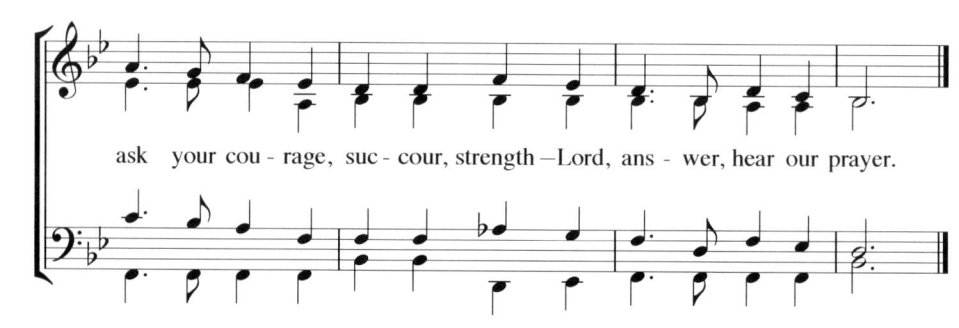

1. For those who strive for justice and make a stand for good, who strive to give the poor a chance to live life as they should, for all who labour, heart and soul, to make our world more fair, we ask your courage, succour, strength—Lord, answer, hear our prayer.

Text © Copyright 2006 Kevin Mayhew Ltd.
*It is illegal to photocopy music.*

2. For those who show compassion,
   who work to heal and mend,
   who nurse the sick, support the weak,
   encourage and befriend,
   for all who reach out in your name
   to offer love and care,
   we ask your blessing, power, help —
   Lord, answer, hear our prayer.

3. For those who tackle conflict,
   where wounds run red and raw,
   who strive to conquer hate and fear
   and put a stop to war,
   who work to foster dialogue
   despite the scars we bear,
   we ask your guidance, vision, faith —
   Lord, answer, hear our prayer.

4. For those who try to witness
   to Christ through word and deed,
   to show his love embraces all,
   each colour, race and creed,
   who point to light and life and hope
   in which we all can share,
   we ask your wisdom, grace and truth —
   Lord, answer, hear our prayer.

*Songs for a*
SERVANT
CHURCH

# 32  Forgive us when our deeds ignore

Martin E. Leckebusch (b.1962)                                      Samuel Webbe (1740-1816)

MELCOMBE LM

1. Forgive us when our deeds ignore your righteous rule of all the earth, when our decisions harm the poor, denying their eternal worth.

2. Forgive us when we turn aside
from what is honest, true and fair,
when dreams of pleasure, wealth and pride
supplant your clear commands to care.

3. Forgive us, Lord, our endless greed
for what was never truly ours,
when, driven more by want than need,
we harness this world's brutal pow'rs.

4. Forgive us that we change the rules
by which the game of life is played,
and never learn to wield the tools
which could see joy and hope remade.

5. Forgive us, God! Our lives betray
our shallow, vague response to grace;
so help us walk your holy way,
to make your world a better place.

Words: © Copyright Martin Leckebusch/administered by The Jubilate Group.
www.jubilate.co.uk. Used by permission.
*It is illegal to photocopy music.*

## 33 From a manger in a stable

Jean Holloway (b.1939)　　　　　　　　　　　　　　　　　　　　Colin Mawby (b.1936)

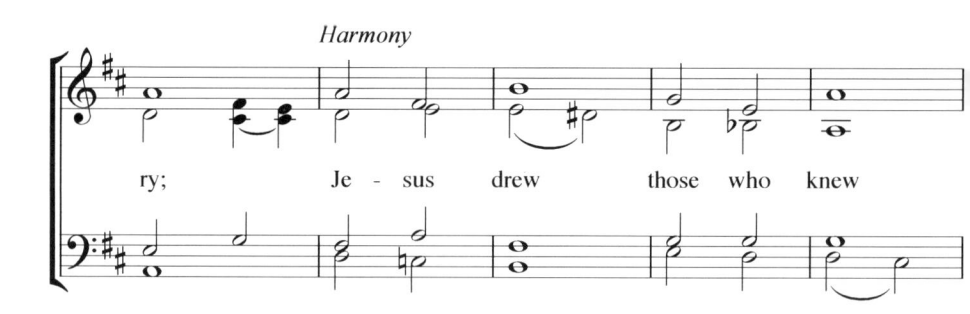

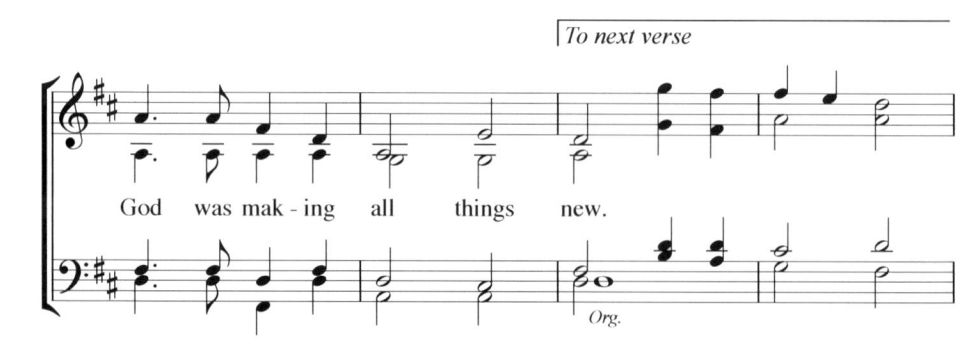

MANSFIELD 87 87 67

1. From a manger in a stable, to a cross on Calvary; from a star's illumination, to a night of treachery; Jesus drew those who knew God was making all things new.

*© Copyright 2000 Kevin Mayhew Ltd.*
*It is illegal to photocopy music.*

2. Christ, whose words of admonition
   calmed the Sea of Galilee,
   still this world of stormy conflict,
   reconcile your family;
   show a way to allay
   war and violence today.

3. Those who dared to touch your garment
   found their faith had made them whole;
   touch me with your healing presence,
   send your spirit to console;
   then impart healing art
   to my willing hands and heart.

4. Christ, who fasted in the desert
   and withstood temptation's lure,
   hold me when I start to waver,
   give me guidance when unsure;
   I so long, to be strong,
   yet I do things which are wrong.

5. Christ who feels my ev'ry sorrow,
   Christ who faces all my fears,
   soothe my pain and quench my anguish
   with the cleansing gift of tears;
   meet me where my despair
   seems impossible to bear.

6. From the solemn final supper
   in a quiet upper room,
   to the glorious resurrection
   signalled by the empty tomb;
   Christ my Lord, life outpoured,
   and the reign of Love restored.

# Songs *for a* Servant Church

# 34 From near and far

Jean Holloway (b.1939)　　　　　　　　　　　　　　　　Alan Rees (1941-2005)

CREATION'S LORD DCM

1. From near and far, from East and West, we gather in this place
to celebrate the one true Lord of ev'ry tongue and race.
With open minds and willing hearts, we come prepared to share,
rejoicing in the fellowship of laughter, song and pray'r.

2. Entrusted with community
through which the church can speak,
we tell the world of Christ, whose reign
empow'rs the poor and weak.
The church on earth, divided, flawed,
is yet a living sign
of how the broken, touched by grace,
discloses the divine.

3. Prepared to listen and forgive,
together we will grow
in unity that comes of God
from whom all blessings flow.
When we must leave this fellowship
and go forth in his name,
we pray that Christ will send us out
with hearts of love aflame.

© Copyright 2000 Kevin Mayhew Ltd.
*It is illegal to photocopy music.*

# 35 From opposite directions

Lucy Berry (b.1957)  Samuel Sebastian Wesley (1810-1876)

AURELIA 76 76 D

1. From opposite directions two great processions came;
one in the name of Power, one in Salvation's name.
One from Oppression's palace beneath an emp'ror's thumb.
The other from the people, the village and the slum.

Text © Copyright 2014 Kevin Mayhew Ltd.
*It is illegal to photocopy music.*

2. From opposite directions
   rode Pontius Pilate in,
   expediency's servant,
   the willing slave of sin;
   and Jesus Christ, a servant
   to love which never dies,
   to God, to us, to Meaning,
   to dreadful sacrifice.

3. From opposite directions
   they rode from east and west;
   God on a borrowed donkey
   and Rome its pure-bred best,
   while two great crowds of people
   applauded in one breath
   the brutish might of bullies
   or love which conquers death.

4. From opposite directions
   we still are called today.
   We choose to join with power —
   or take the other Way;
   while some wave palms and worship,
   declare we're Jesus' friend,
   yet disappear, like magic,
   before the bitter end.

# 36 From the heart of God the Father

Christopher Massey

Plainsong melody (13th century)
adapt. by Theodoricus Petrus
in 'Piae Cantiones' (1582)

**CORDE NATUS (DIVINUM MYSTERIUM)** 87 87 87 7

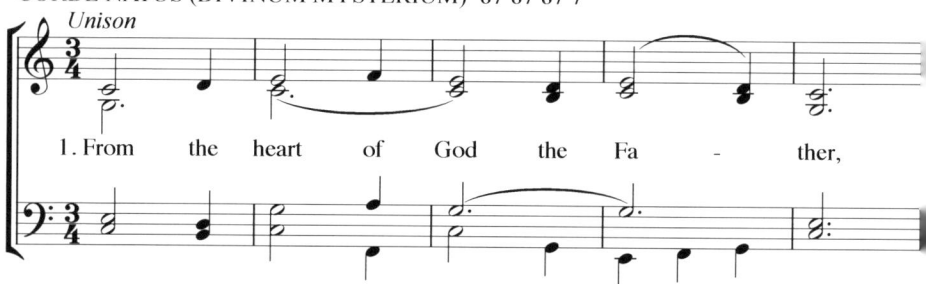

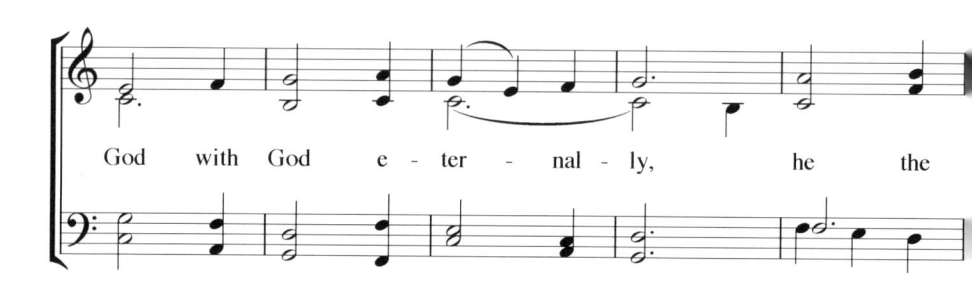

*Unison*

1. From the heart of God the Father,
God with God eternally,
he the Source and he the Ending
of all things that came to be;
all that was, and is, and

Text © Copyright 2014 Kevin Mayhew Ltd.
*It is illegal to photocopy music.*

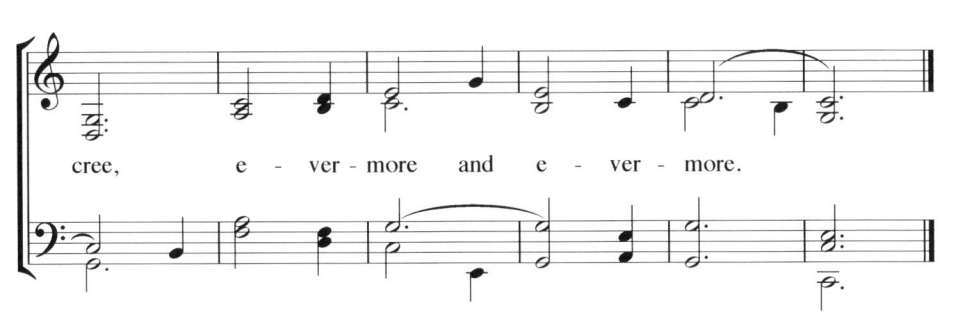

*[music: ...will be, comes to birth by his decree, evermore and evermore.]*

2. From his word sprang all beginnings:
   light began creation's day,
   sun and moon, the earth and heavens,
   planets circling on their way;
   all that lives and grows within it,
   life and hope in joyful play,
   evermore and evermore.

3. Blessed is that day for ever,
   joy in heav'n and hope on earth,
   when, by grace, the Virgin mother
   brought the Son to mortal birth,
   by the Spirit's pow'r conferring
   on us all God's seal of worth,
   evermore and evermore.

4. Angels in the heights, adore him,
   heav'n and earth with glory blaze,
   pow'rs and empires bow before him,
   singing his eternal praise;
   and, in harmony united,
   let us all our voices raise,
   evermore and evermore.

5. This is he whom ancient prophets,
   by the Spirit's pow'r, foretold;
   he whose word of hope was written
   in the holy books of old;
   now to him be praise and glory,
   more than earth can ever hold,
   evermore and evermore.

6. Let the universe sing glory
   to the Father and the Son,
   with the Holy Spirit reigning,
   fully Three and wholly One;
   and the song of praise re-echo
   while eternal ages run,
   evermore and evermore.

## 37 From the heights of glory

*What a gift*

Susie Hare

Susie Hare (b.1947)

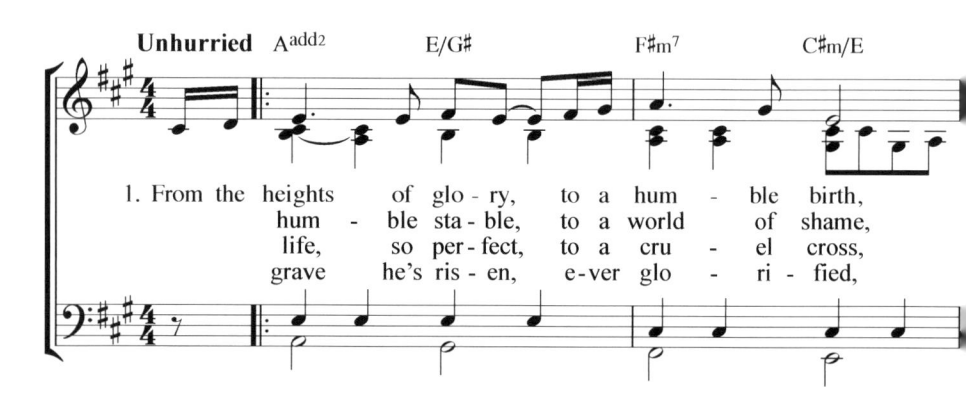

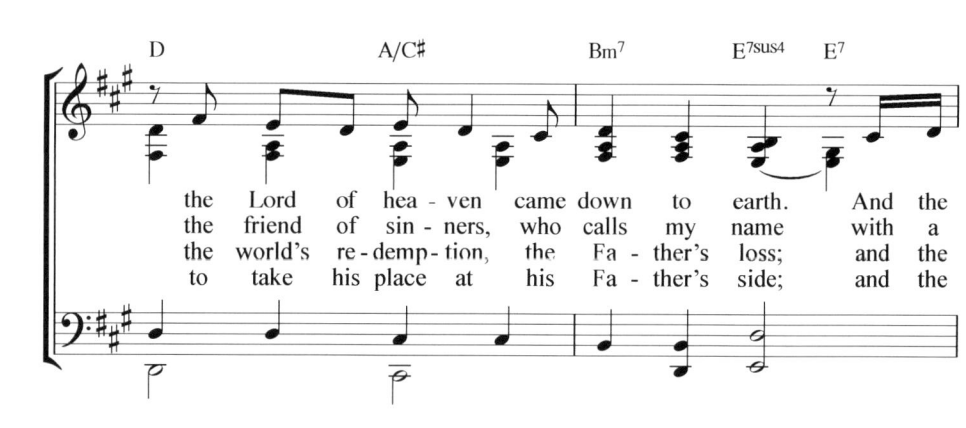

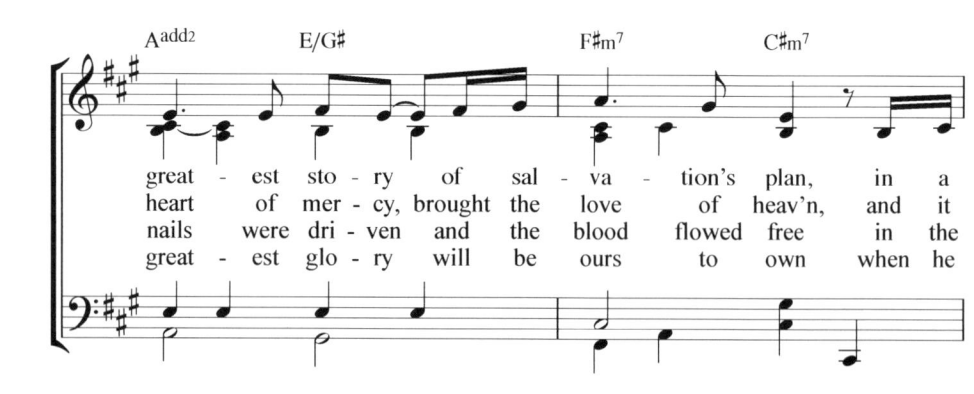

1. From the heights of glory, to a humble birth, the Lord of heaven came down to earth. And the greatest story of salvation's plan, in a heart of mercy, brought the love of heav'n, and it

2. From humble stable, to a world of shame, the friend of sinners, who calls my name with a nails were driven and the blood flowed free in the

3. From life, so perfect, to a cruel cross, the world's redemption, the Father's loss; and the

4. From grave he's risen, ever glorified, to take his place at his Father's side; and the greatest glory will be ours to own when he

© Copyright 2001 Kevin Mayhew Ltd.
*It is illegal to photocopy music.*

sta - ble room be - gan.
gave lives hope a - gain.
hands out - stretched for me.
comes to take us home. What a

gift, what a gift we are giv - en; sa - cri-

fice of the Fa - ther for us. What a

gift, what a gift we are giv - en; King of

*To next verse*

kings, Lord of lords, Je - sus!
2. From a
3. From a
4. From the

*Last time*

sus! What a hope, what a hope we are given; sacrifice of the Father for us. What a song, to proclaim 'He is risen!' King of kings, Lord of lords, Jesus! King of kings, Lord of lords, Jesus!

*Songs for a*
SERVANT
CHURCH

# 38 Give me a heart that will honour you

Martin E. Leckebusch (b.1962)          Kevin Mayhew (b.1942)

RATTLESDEN 9 10 10 9 10 10 10 extended

1. Give me a heart that will honour you: in willing submission before your throne, ambitions and plans to be yours alone; give me a heart that will honour you: will follow the way to the Saviour's cross, ac-

© Copyright 2013 Kevin Mayhew Ltd.
*It is illegal to photocopy music.*

cept-ing the chal-lenge of pain and loss — oh, give me a heart that will hon-our you: will hon-our, hon-our you.

2. Give me a heart that will honour you:
a heart that is rich in humility,
a heart that will worship eternally;
give me a heart that will honour you:
no more can my emptiness stay concealed —
my twisted emotions to you I yield;
oh, give me a heart that will honour you,
will honour, honour you.

3. Give me a heart that will honour you:
rejecting the dazzle of wealth and fame,
continually living to praise your name;
give me a heart that will honour you
where patience and kindness can freely grow,
enabling the pow'r of your love to flow —
oh, give me a heart that will honour you,
will honour, honour you.

*Songs for a Servant Church*

# 39 God beyond earth's finest treasures

Martin E. Leckebusch (b.1962)  
based on Psalm 16

George Clement Martin (1844-1916)

ST HELEN 87 87 87

1. God beyond earth's finest treasures, you alone shall have my praise; I will love your cherished people, I will serve you all my days; be my ruler, be my refuge, God the guardian of my ways.

2. You have caused my life to prosper —
countless gifts your love has planned!
Day and night your wisdom prompts me,
shows me all that you command;
God before me, God beside me,
safe within your care I stand.

3. When my earthly days are over,
fresh delights remain in store:
vaster riches, fuller pleasures
than I ever knew before —
life unending, joy unfading
in your presence evermore.

© Copyright 2001 Kevin Mayhew Ltd.  
*It is illegal to photocopy music.*

# 40 God has called us to a journey

Nick Fawcett (b.1957)  June Nixon

CASTLEMAINE 87 87 D

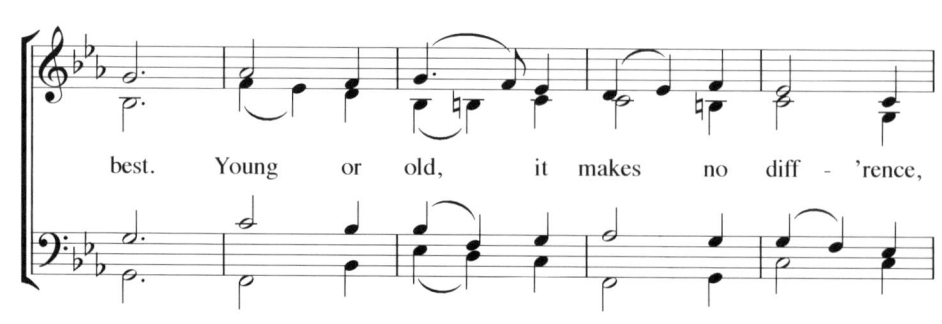

1. God has called us to a jour-ney, to a ne-ver-end-ing quest; al-ways seek-ing new ho-ri-zons, al-ways search-ing for the best. Young or old, it makes no diff-'rence,

Text © Copyright 2000, and Music © Copyright 1992 Kevin Mayhew Ltd.
*It is illegal to photocopy music.*

still the journey's just begun, keep us looking to the future, never dream the race is run.

2. Let the search for truth continue,
   may its flame for ever burn —
   what we know is only partial,
   there is more we need to learn.
   Do not fear what seems to challenge,
   do not cling to what is dead.
   Let the voice of God disturb you —
   by the way of Christ be led.

3. Faith must always be evolving,
   if it is to stay alive.
   Never viewed as our possession,
   nor a place where we arrive.
   God has called us to a journey,
   always asking one step more.
   Trust in him and keep believing
   that he holds the best in store.

# 41 God has promised many things

Martin E. Leckebusch (b.1962)  
Joseph Parry (1841-1903)

ABERYSTWYTH 77 77 D

1. God has pro-mised ma-ny things— trea-sures from a heav'n-ly store;
now in Christ the e-cho sounds: 'Yes' to all he said be-fore.
Think of how he gave his Son— such a pre-cious gift in-deed!
How will he not al-so give all that we could e-ver need?

Text © Copyright 1999 Kevin Mayhew Ltd.  
*It is illegal to photocopy music.*

2. Faith unlocks the pow'r of God
   in the face of doubt and fear;
   access to his throne is ours —
   what can stop us drawing near?
   God has pledged to hear our pray'rs
   when we ask in Jesus' name,
   so we come with eager hearts
   and his promise boldly claim.

3. Faith enjoys the peace of God —
   freedom from anxiety!
   What can earthly riches give?
   Christ is our security!
   Faith will therefore never cling
   to the wealth we now possess,
   but will find the better way —
   giving freely, keeping less.

4. God has promised many things —
   treasures from a heav'nly store;
   now in Christ the echo sounds:
   'Yes' to all he said before.
   So we raise a loud 'Amen!'
   as we make his word our own
   and, with faith to guide our lives,
   make his promised riches known.

# 42 God is our strength from days of old

Michael Forster (b.1946)  
Melody from 'Geistliche Lieder', Wittenberg (1535)

LUTHER 87 87 8 87

1. God is our strength from days of old, the hope of ev-'ry na-tion, whose pow'r con-ceived the u-ni-verse and set the earth's foun-da-tion; though hid-den from our mor-tal sight in realms of un-cre-

*Text © Copyright 2014 Kevin Mayhew Ltd.*  
*It is illegal to photocopy music.*

a - ted light, yet known through-out cre - a - tion.

2. That Word of life, before all things
   in primal darkness spoken,
   became for us the Word made flesh,
   for our redemption broken.
   For us he set his pow'r aside,
   for us was mocked and crucified
   and then to glory woken.

3. That Breath of God, who brooded first
   upon the new creation,
   who lit with light the virgin's womb
   to bear the world's salvation;
   the Spirit of eternal grace
   now calls the world of time and space
   to hope and liberation.

4. O great Creator, Spirit Word,
   the well-spring of creation,
   our Alpha and our Omega,
   our hope and our salvation;
   to Father, Holy Spirit, Son,
   mysterious Three for ever one,
   be praise and adoration.

# 43 God of life, we come in worship

Nick Fawcett (b.1957)　　　　　　　　　　　　　　　　Kevin Mayhew (b.1942)

BRETTENHAM 87 87 D

1. God of life, we come in worship, lost in wonder, filled with awe. At your feet we kneel in homage, here to marvel and adore. Words cannot express your greatness, awesome is your majesty: higher than the highest mountain, deeper than the deepest

© Copyright 2013 Kevin Mayhew Ltd.
*It is illegal to photocopy music.*

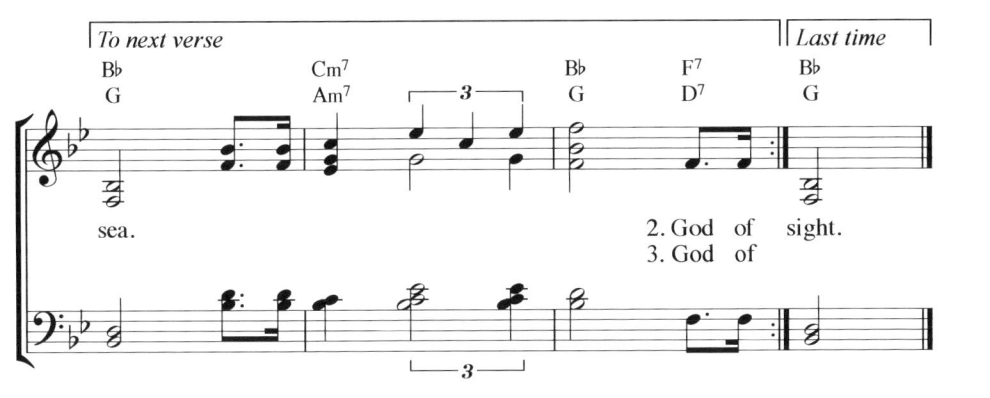

2. God of love, we come rejoicing,
    here to celebrate your grace.
    Consecrate this sacred moment,
    help us meet you face to face.
    In the love of Christ enfold us,
    by his touch make us anew:
    cleanse, renew, restore, refashion
    all we are and all we do.

3. God of light, we come in gladness,
    souls on fire and hearts ablaze,
    reaching out in adoration,
    singing hymns and songs of praise.
    Take the hope that flames within us,
    take the joy that burns so bright;
    may our lives reflect your glory,
    finding favour in your sight.

# 44 God of love

Jean Holloway (b.1939)

Edward Elgar (1857-1934)
arr. Donald Thomson

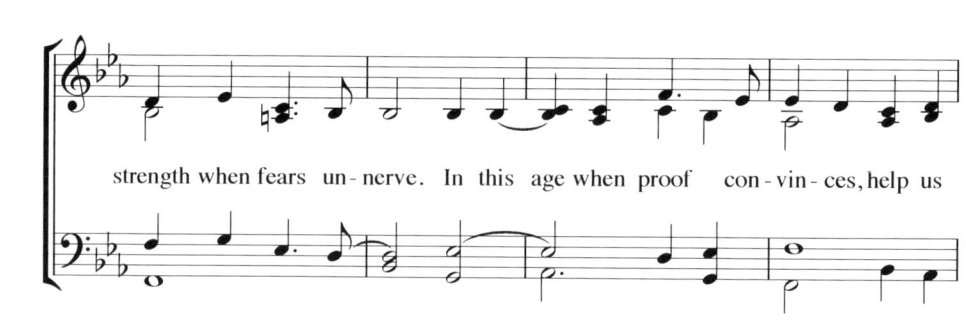

AVE VERUM 87 87 D

1. God of love, you freely give us blessings more than we deserve; be our light in times of darkness, be our strength when fears un-nerve. In this age when proof convinces, help us see where wisdom lies; more enduring than per-

Text © Copyright 1999, and this music arrangement
© Copyright 2014 Kevin Mayhew Ltd.
*It is illegal to photocopy music.*

sua - sion is the truth which ne - ver lies.

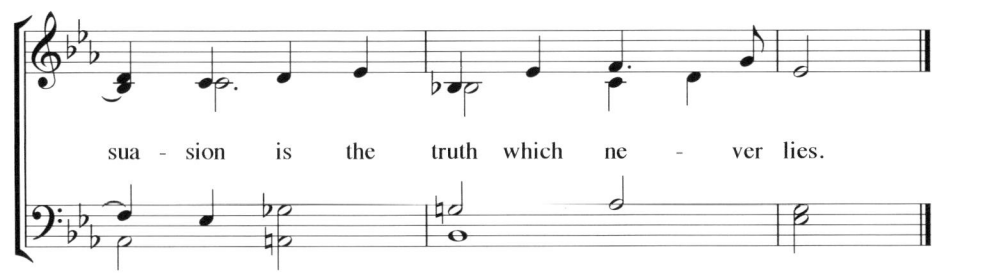

2. Son incarnate, yours the presence
which can heal an aching heart;
over death you reign triumphant,
you alone new life impart.
From your birth so long awaited,
to the cross on Calvary,
you will serve as our example,
let us, Lord, your servants be.

3. Holy Spirit, inspiration
day by day, yet mystery;
with the Son and the Creator
you form mystic unity.
Draw us into your communion,
with the love that sets us free;
bind our hearts to you for ever,
holy, blessèd Trinity.

# 45 God of present, God of past

Nick Fawcett (b.1957)

George Frederick Root (1820-1895)
arr. Donald Thomson

**TRAMP! TRAMP! TRAMP!  77 11 77 11 and Refrain**

1. God of pre-sent, God of past, God the first and God the last, God of all that is and was and yet shall be, hear the prai-ses that we bring, hear the grate-ful songs we sing for your faith-ful-ness through-out our his-to-ry.

Text and this music arrangement
© Copyright 2014 Kevin Mayhew Ltd.
*It is illegal to photocopy music.*

**Refrain**

Year by year your hand has guided, led our people on their way. God of present, God of past, God the first and God the last, hear the worship that we offer you today.

2. For the memories we share,
   living record of your care,
   for the work of Christ in centuries gone by,
   Lord, receive our thanks we pray,
   help us walk in turn your way
   that the legacy you give will never die.

3. Like your people here of old
   give us vision, make us bold,
   grant us help and strength, like them, to run our race.
   Take the service we would give,
   take the lives we long to live,
   work within our hearts your miracle of grace.

4. Each decision that we make,
   ev'ry step of faith we take,
   may it build upon the work that's gone before.
   Conscious of the debt we owe,
   may we help your kingdom grow,
   play our part in all you hold as yet in store.

# 46 God of the nations

Michael Forster (b.1946)  Henri Friedrich Hémy (1818-1888)

ST CATHERINE (TYNEMOUTH) 88 88 88

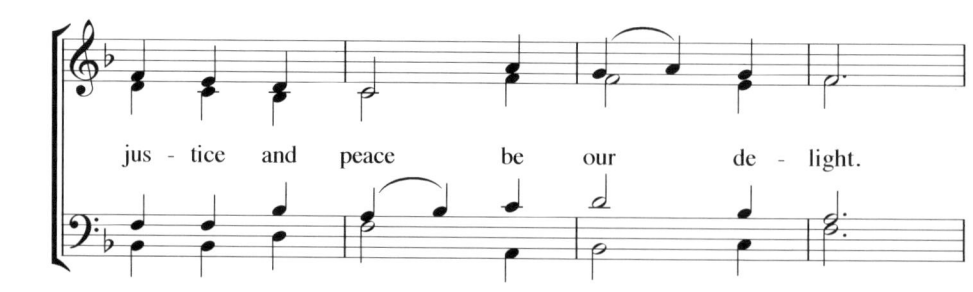

1. God of the nations, hear our prayer
from warring pride your people spare;
let us in love and truth unite,
justice and peace be our delight.

Text © Copyright 2014 Kevin Mayhew Ltd.
*It is illegal to photocopy music.*

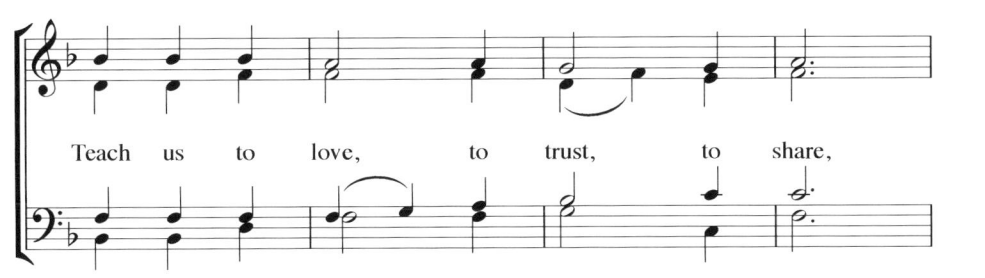

Teach us to love, to trust, to share,
God of the nations, hear our prayer.

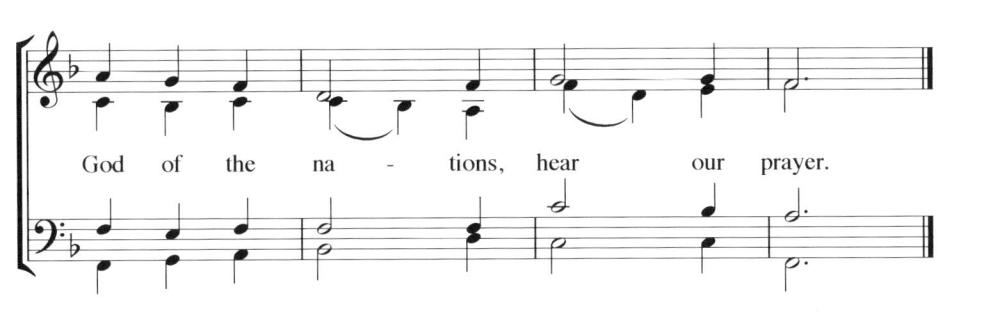

2. Father, forgive the nations' rage,
   prejudice passed from age to age,
   banners made sacred, life made cheap,
   widows and orphans left to weep.
   When we in spiteful fears engage,
   Father, forgive the nations' rage.

3. Here may we venerate our dead,
   building the peace for which they bled,
   never to make their dying vain,
   sending their youth to die again.
   When no more needless blood is shed,
   then shall we venerate our dead.

4. Teach us to turn our bombs to bread,
   help us to see the hungry fed,
   welcome the diff"rent, cease to blame,
   justice and peace for all proclaim.
   So that all people might be fed,
   teach us to turn our bombs to bread.

# 47 Good Joseph was a man

Lucy Berry (b.1957)

Malcolm Archer (b.1953)

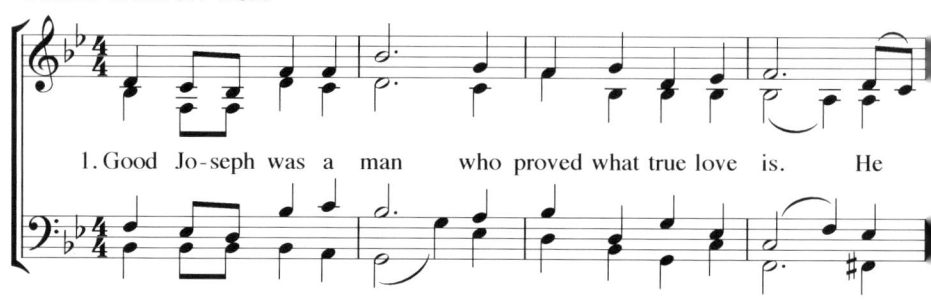

COURT BARTON DSM

1. Good Joseph was a man who proved what true love is. He took on someone else's son and brought him up as his. He saw what should be done and knew he must begin. I want to be as loving and as practical as him.

Text © Copyright 2014 and Music © Copyright 1999 Kevin Mayhew Ltd.
*It is illegal to photocopy music.*

2. He showed the growing Christ
   whilst he was just a boy
   how we can bear another's pain
   or share another's joy:
   and carry on our backs
   responsibility
   beyond what anyone could ask,
   and do it lovingly.

3. We thank you, Christ, for work
   which others have begun;
   hard, heavy, selfless, loving jobs
   which haven't yet been done;
   and thank you for those folk
   the ones who have the grace
   to see and know what should be done
   and do it in Christ's place.

# 48 Good Lord, deliver us

Barbara Glasson

Rod Boucher
arr. Marian Hellen

**Bold stomp**

*Refrain*

Good Lord, de-liv-er us this side of Pa-ra-dise.

Let us live fair-ly this side of Pa-ra-dise,

so on-ly peace will pre-vail.

*Fine* | *To verses*

1. From the lure of cor-

© Copyright 2015 Kevin Mayhew Ltd.
*It is illegal to photocopy music.*

rup - tion to bribe our own ends and the
long - ing for pow'r to de - feat.

2. From the impulse to shove in ahead of the race
   and then cheating to reach the first place.

3. From the need to suceed at whatever the cost
   and a sense of defeat if we fail.

4. From the push for more land to stake out a fresh claim
   and the need to protect our own rights.

5. From creating more guns in the face of our fear,
   we are forging more weapons of hate.

6. From a faith that insists it has all of the truth,
   and heaven's restricted to us.

# 49 Gracious God, in adoration

Basil Bridge (b.1927)             Malcolm Archer (b.1952)

GOULDSBROOK 87 87 87

1. Gracious God, in adoration saints with joy before you fall; only when our hearts are leaden can we fail to hear their call: 'Come with wonder, serve with gladness God whose pow'r created all.'

© Copyright 1999 Kevin Mayhew Ltd.
*It is illegal to photocopy music.*

2. Earth and sky in silent praises
   speak to those with eyes to see;
   all earth's living creatures echo
   'God has made us!' So may we
   come with wonder, serve with gladness
   him through whom they came to be.

3. You have made us in your image,
   breathed your Spirit, giv'n us birth;
   Jesus calls, whose cross has given
   ev'ry life eternal worth,
   'Come with wonder, serve with gladness,
   let God's will be done on earth!'

4. Earth by war and want is threatened;
   deep the roots of fear and greed;
   let your mercy be our measure
   as we see our neighbour's need,
   come with wonder, serve with gladness,
   share your gift of daily bread.

5. Holy Spirit, urging, striving,
   give us love that casts out fear,
   courage, seeking peace with justice,
   faith to make this message clear —
   'Come with wonder, serve with gladness,
   live in hope; the Lord is near!'

# 50 Hallelu, hallelu, hallelujah

James Wright

James Wright
arr. Donald Thomson

-ry in Beth-le-hem, in a
hill-side in Beth-le-hem, when a
way to Beth-le-hem, from the

dus-ty sta-ble with a low-ly cra-dle in Beth-le-hem.
host of an-gels start-ed sing-ing prai-ses in Beth-le-hem.
O-ri-ent to the land of Is-rael to Beth-le-hem.

And all the a-ni-mals stand-ing in the straw must have
And the night lit up with an awe-some sight and the
And the star shone bright in the sky that night to

won-dered who he was, was he just the son of a
shep-herds looked a-mazed, but the an-gel said, 'Please
show them where to go, so that they may bring gifts

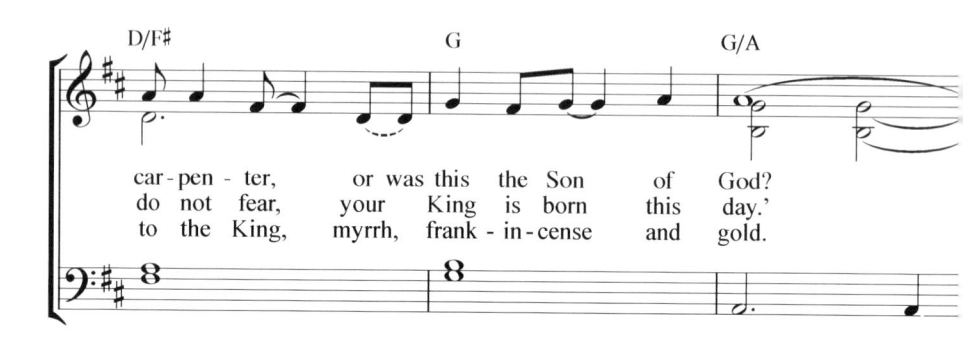

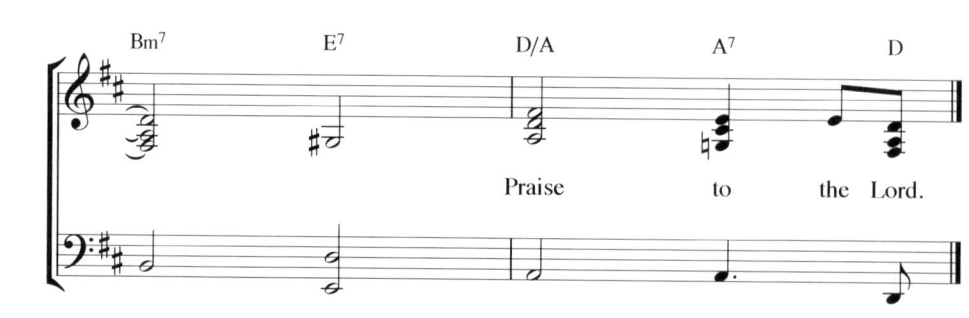

carpenter, or was this the Son of God?
do not fear, your King is born this day.'
to the King, myrrh, frankincense and gold.

Refrain *D.S.*

Halle-

*CODA*

praise to the Lord. Praise to the Lord

Praise to the Lord.

# 51 Hallelujah

*Hallelujah Chorus*

Charles Jennens (1700-1773)

George Frideric Handel (1685-1759)
adapted and arr. Donald Thomson

Hal-le-lu-jah, hal-le-lu-jah, hal-le-lu-jah, hal-le-lu-jah, hal-le-lu-jah. And he shall reign for e-ver and e-ver. King of kings and Lord of lords. Hal-le-lu-jah, hal-le-lu-jah, hal-le-lu-jah, hal-le-lu-jah, hal-le-lu-jah!

**Slower**

This music adaptation and arrangement
© Copyright 2014 Kevin Mayhew Ltd.
*It is illegal to photocopy music.*

## 52 Happy to share
Garth Hewitt

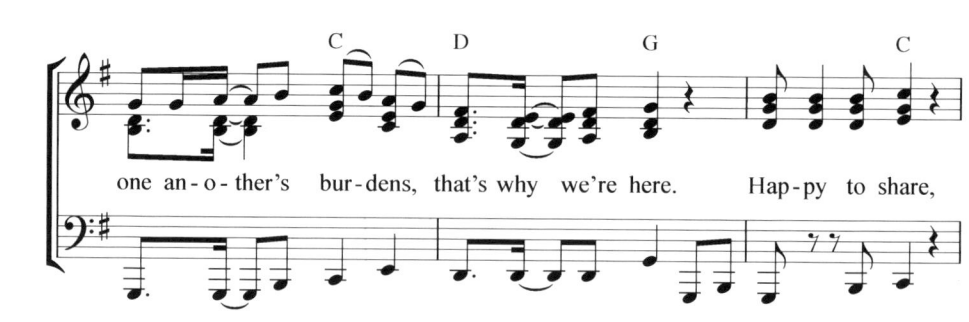

## That's why we're here
Garth Hewitt

*Refrain*
Happy to share, happy to bear one another's burdens, that's why we're here. Happy to share, happy to bear one another's burdens, that's why we're here.

*Last time, repeat Refrain ad lib.*
*Fine*

© Copyright 2012 Kevin Mayhew Ltd.
*It is illegal to photocopy music.*

1. We are made in the i-mage of God, that's why we're here. We're
told to walk where Je-sus trod, that's why we're here.
Feed-ing the hun-gry and heal-ing the lame, that's why we're here.
Do-ing it all in Je-sus' name, that's why we're here.

2. Reach out your hand and help your brother,
that's why we're here.
Reach out your hand and help your sister,
that's why we're here.
Work for justice and work for peace,
that's why we're here.
Work for Jesus 'til this life cease,
that's why we're here.

# 53 He broke the rules

Garth Hewitt  Garth Hewitt

($\quarter = 130$)

1. He broke the rules when he spoke to you. To show you your va-lue when he spoke to you. He saw deep and he saw your thirst: but love came

© Copyright 2012 Kevin Mayhew Ltd.
*It is illegal to photocopy music.*

Refrain
G7 C F
first so he broke the rules. He broke the rules when he
C G7 C
spoke to you. Hope broke through when he spoke to
C7 F C
you. The dis - ci - ples were a - mazed when he spoke to
Am Dm G7 F
you be - cause love broke through when he broke the
C Dm G7 F C
Fine
rules. 2. He broke

rul - es of gen-der, re - li - gion and race;
showed you your dig - ni - ty right to your face. A
re - vo - lu - tion start - ed as he spoke to you. Oh
he broke the rules and then love broke through.

*Refrain*
He broke the rules when he spoke to you.

Hope broke through when he spoke to you. The disciples were amazed when he spoke to you because love broke through when he broke the rules.

## 54 Hear our prayer for others

Nick Fawcett (b.1957)        Malcolm Archer (b.1952)

VICARS' CLOSE 65 65 D

1. Hear our prayer for others in the trials they face — fellow sisters, brothers: grant to all your grace. Heal the crushed and broken, body, mind and soul — let your word be spoken, touch and make them whole.

© Copyright 1999 Kevin Mayhew Ltd.
*It is illegal to photocopy music.*

2. Challenge rich and greedy,
   strengthen the oppressed,
   reach out to the needy,
   comfort the distressed.
   May the humble flourish,
   may the poor be fed,
   in your mercy nourish
   all who crave for bread.

3. Bring to ev'ry nation
   harmony once more,
   reconciliation,
   peace instead of war.
   Hear our intercession,
   make our life a prayer;
   help us give expression
   to your love and care.

# 55 Hold tight

Barbara Glasson

Rod Boucher
arr. Marian Hellen

**Driving and slippery**

1. Hold tight with both hands to all that is good, keep firm with your feet on the shifting sand.

© Copyright 2015 Kevin Mayhew Ltd.
*It is illegal to photocopy music.*

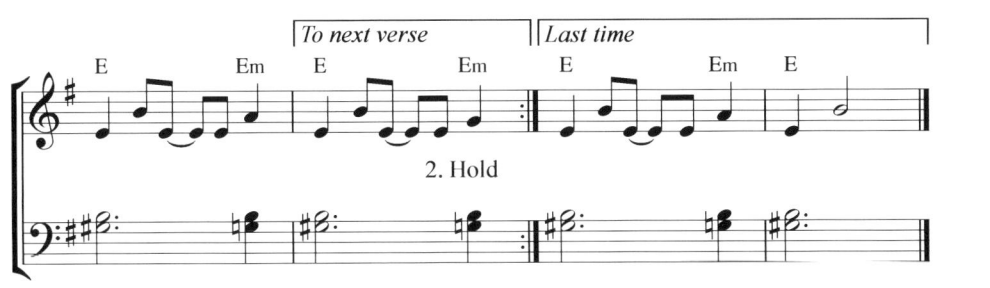

2. Hold out for the strength to continue to cope,
   avoid the bleak lies that the gossips speak.

3. Hold firm to your nerve when the road is bleak,
   let your hope survive 'til you're understood.

4. Hold fast with your grip on the slippery slope,
   keep facing the light of the nearest coast.

5. Hold on for the time when the weak can boast
   of a life well lived when the love ran deep.

# 56 How amazing

Susie Hare

Susie Hare (b.1947)

**Brightly** (♩ = 138)

How a-ma-zing are you Lord, how re-deem-ing is your blood, how sus-tain-ing is the grace

© Copyright 2015 Kevin Mayhew Ltd.
*It is illegal to photocopy music.*

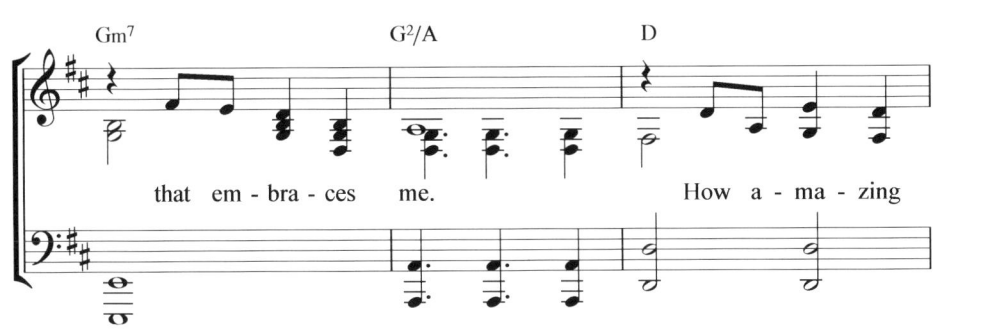

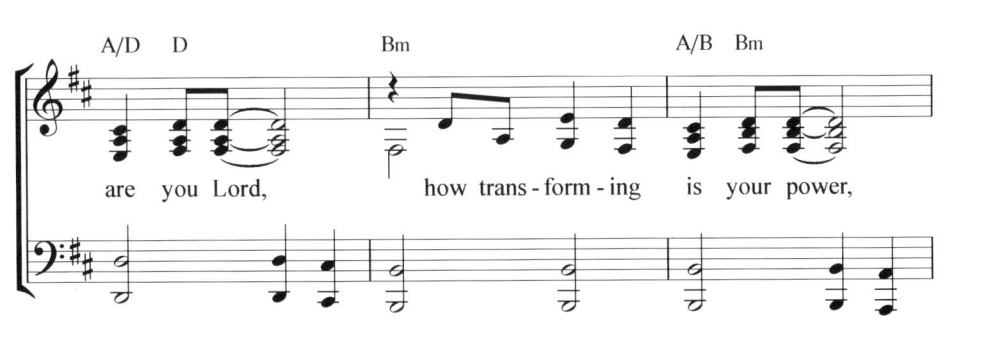

that em-bra-ces me. How a-ma-zing are you Lord, how trans-form-ing is your power, how un-chan-ging is your love, pour-ing out so free. Ev-'ry hour, ev-'ry day, your good-ness is just the same. Ev-'ry-where, ev-'ry way, a-gain and a-gain. I will sing of your faith-ful-ness, I will sing of the things you do, I will sing of the gift

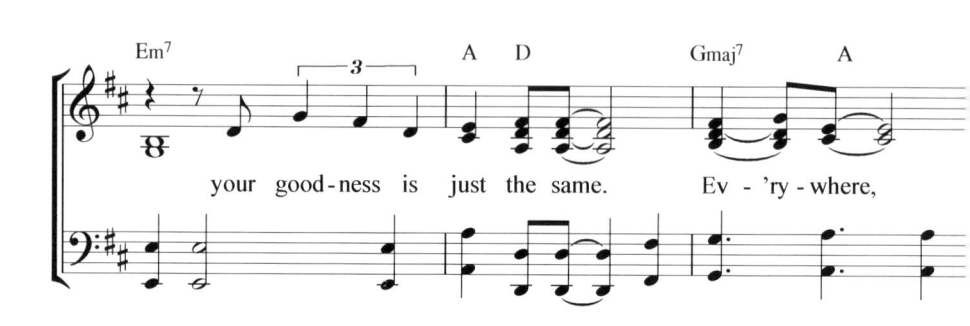

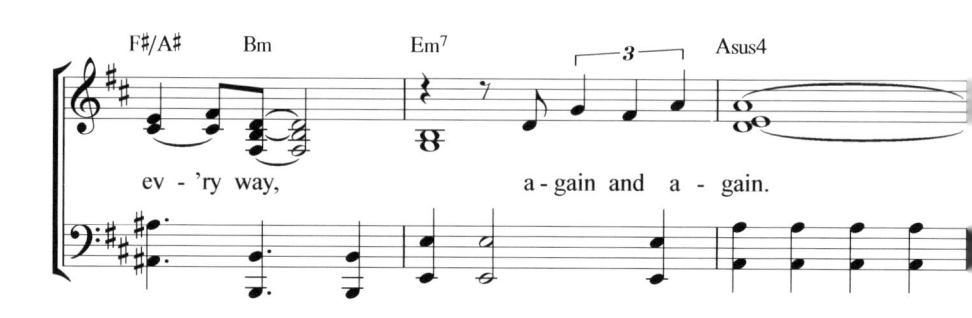

D/F♯ Em Asus4 A
of grace that gives me life in you.
D A/C♯ Bm
All my bless-ings are un - de-served, all my weak-ness-es you
D/A G D/F♯
can see; but your foun-tain is un - re-served in
Em7 G/A D D2 D
pour - ing out to me.

# 57 How did you feel, Lord Jesus

Nick Fawcett (b.1957)

Hans Leo Hassler (1564-1612)
harm. Johann Sebastian Bach

PASSION CHORALE 65 65 D

1. How did you feel, Lord Jesus, when first you heard the call — when sud-den-ly you rea-lised you'd give your life for all? Did you be-gin to won-der if you could see it through, or

Text © Copyright 2000 Kevin Mayhew Ltd.
*It is illegal to photocopy music.*

were you sure already no other way would do?

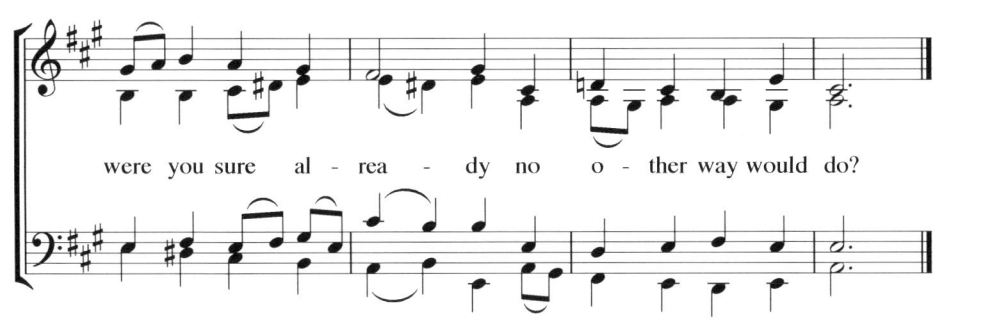

2. How did you feel, Lord Jesus,
   when you sat down to dine
   and shared with your disciples
   a meal of bread and wine?
   You knew one would betray you,
   and one his faith deny.
   How could you still be ready
   to give your all and die?

3. How did you feel, Lord Jesus,
   when on the cross you bled —
   your body cruelly broken
   and thorns pressed on your head?
   That cry of 'It is finished!' —
   what was it meant to say?
   Was it a shout of vict'ry
   or protest of dismay?

4. How did you feel, Lord Jesus,
   when, rising from the tomb,
   you found the scared disciples
   locked in an upper room?
   Was that a disappointment,
   or did you understand
   how hard they must have found it
   to grasp your death was planned?

5. I cannot tell, Lord Jesus,
   just what you faced each day;
   how much it must have cost you
   to walk your chosen way.
   But what I need to ponder,
   and what you want to know,
   is have I heard your challenge
   and does my answer show?

# 58 How rich and deep God's judgements are

Martin E. Leckebusch (b.1962)  
Henri Friedrich Hémy (1814-1888)

IVER 86 86 D

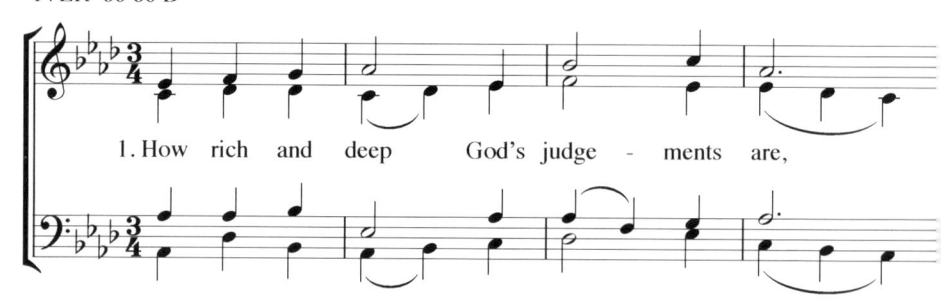

1. How rich and deep God's judgements are, his knowledge, how profound! Who understands the path he takes? His wisdom, who can sound? If we should try to

*Text © Copyright 2000 Kevin Mayhew Ltd.*  
*It is illegal to photocopy music.*

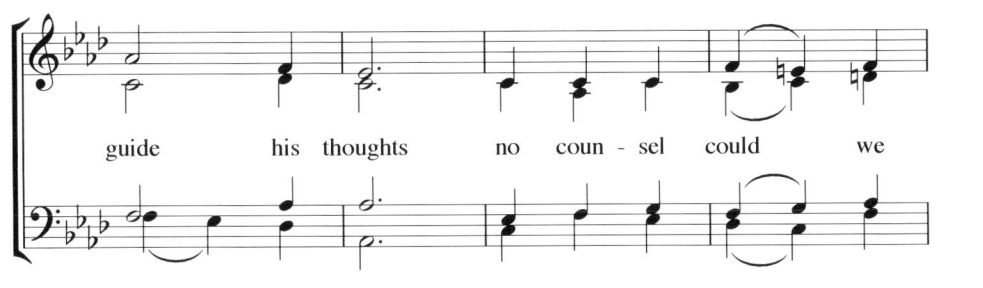

*guide his thoughts no coun-sel could we find to of-fer the all-see-ing One who forms both heart and mind.*

May also be sung to 'Kingsfold'

2. And who can give him anything
which he must then repay,
or charge a debt to his account
against the judgement day?
Eternal glory and renown
shall evermore be his —
the Source of all created things,
the End of all that is!

3. And yet our living sacrifice
this awesome God desires:
our mortal bodies, yielded up,
to serve as he requires!
Such giving is a sacred act,
such worship, pure and right:
the best response of thankful hearts,
and pleasing in his sight.

4. Then by his all-surpassing pow'r
our minds he will transform
to see this world's ungodly ways
no longer as the norm:
for hearts and lives renewed by grace
at last can truly learn
God's good and pleasing will to prove,
his judgements to discern.

## 59 Humble yourselves

Susie Hare

Susie Hare (b.1947)

**Moderate speed**

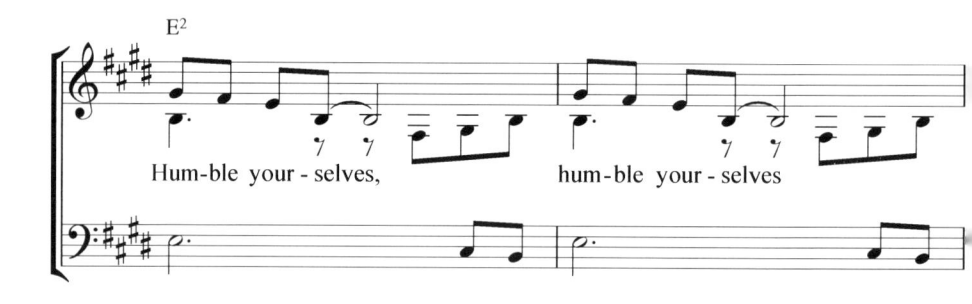

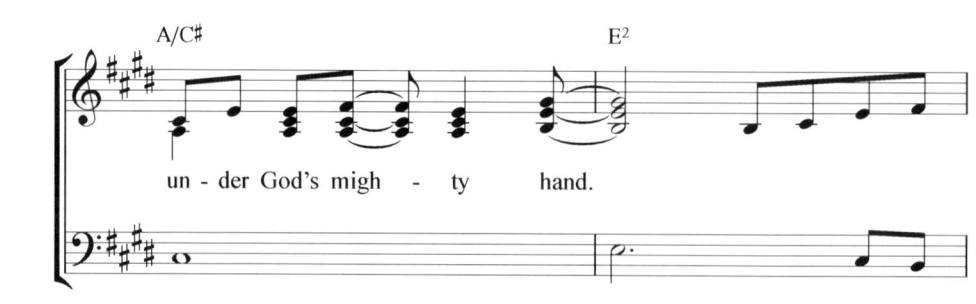

Hum-ble your-selves, hum-ble your-selves un-der God's migh - ty hand.

© Copyright 2001 Kevin Mayhew Ltd.
*It is illegal to photocopy music.*

Hum-ble your-selves and in due time
you will be lift - ed up.
Hum-ble your-selves, hum-ble your-selves
un-der God's migh - ty hand,
cast-ing your care ful - ly on him

be-cause he cares for you. And the God of all grace who called you to glo-ry e-ter-nal in Christ, when suf-fer-ing comes will re-store you and make you strong. To him be the pow - er for e - ver and e - ver. To

him be the pow - er for e - ver. A - men. To

him be the pow - er for e - ver and e - ver. To

him be the pow - er for e - ver. A - men.

*D.C.*

# 60 I lift my eyes to the hills

Susie Hare, based on Psalm 121

Susie Hare (b.1947)

1. I lift my eyes to the hills,
2. And I will trust in the Lord,

I lift my eyes to the hills where does my help
and I will trust in the Lord now and for e-

come from? Where does my help come from?
-ver, now and for e - ver.

© Copyright 2015 Kevin Mayhew Ltd.
*It is illegal to photocopy music.*

My help comes from the Lord.
For his promise is sure,

My help comes from the Lord,
for his promise is sure:
Maker of heaven,
he will watch over me

Maker of earth.
for evermore.

*Refrain*
I will look up to the hills above me,
to the One I know will always love me; he is my strength and

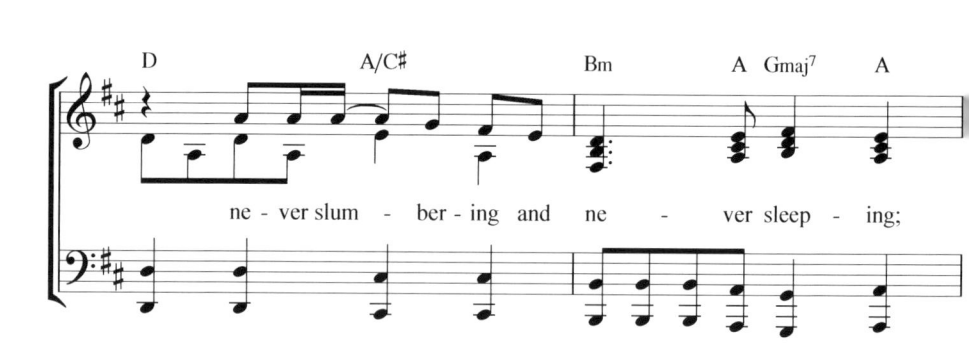

he is my shield and he'll never let me fall.

Day and night he has me in his keeping

never slumbering and never sleeping;

he is my strength and he is my shield and

1.
G9 Gmaj7 A
D G/D
D D7 G/D
he is my all in all.
D G/D
Bm A Gmaj7 A
2.
D
G9
D/F#
He is my strength and he is my shield and
G9 Gmaj7 A
D7 G/D D
he is my all in all.

## 61 I live, dependent on Jesus  *For I can do all things*

Susie Hare  
Susie Hare (b.1947)

86 96 96 87 and Refrain

live, de-pen-dent on Je - sus in ev - 'ry-thing I do, be-ing
sure that he who has pro - mised is faith - ful, good and true. Be-ing
con - fi-dent I'm for - gi - ven and stains of guilt are gone, I
live, se - cure in his keep - ing as my Sa - viour leads me

© Copyright 2015 Kevin Mayhew Ltd.  
*It is illegal to photocopy music.*

Lyrics under the music:

on. For I can do all things in him who strength-ens me. In the power of Je-sus, King of kings, is where my strength shall be.

(2. I be. For I can
3. I

2. I live, dependent on Jesus
   in ev'rything I do,
   being sure, when trouble surrounds me,
   his love surrounds me, too.
   Being confident of his guidance
   wherever I may be,
   my feet are firm on the pathway
   as my Saviour walks with me.

3. I live, dependent on Jesus
   in ev'rything I do,
   being sure that he will sustain me
   in all he takes me through.
   My Saviour is the solid rock
   I build my life upon
   and, by the power of his Spirit,
   in my weakness I am strong.

## 62 I stand on a rock

Susie Hare

Susie Hare (b.1947)

**Brightly**

1. I stand on a rock
2. I walk on a path
3. I live by a grace

that is se - cure,
that is made straight
that set me free

that won't be sha - ken,
by you be - fore me,
from con - dem - na - tion,

© Copyright 2015 Kevin Mayhew Ltd.
*It is illegal to photocopy music.*

for you are a faithful God.

I stand on a promise that is sure,
I walk in a power that keeps firm
I live by a love that won for me

that won't be broken,
my feet beneath me,
a free salvation, for you are a faith-

-ful God.

You're my refuge, strong deliv-'rer, great are the things you've done.
You're my guardian, never sleeping, watching me night and day.
You're the joy that lifts my sadness, faithful in all you do.

You're the mighty, all-sustaining, all-sufficient one.
You're unchanging, you're unfailing, good in ev'ry way.
You're the strength that fills my weakness, I depend on you.

*Refrain* (Refrain twice to end)
Yesterday, today,

Ab Bb Cm Eb/G Ab Cm Bb
G A Bm D/F# G Bm A
for e-ver, you can be re-lied up-on.
Eb Eb/G Ab Bb Cm Eb/G
D D/F# G A Bm D/F#
You will al-ways be my trea-sure, this will al-ways
1, 2.
Fm Ab/Bb Eb Ab Eb/G Fm Ab/Bb Eb
Em G/A D G D/F# Em G/A D
be my song.
3.
Fm Ab/Bb Eb Bb
Em G/A D A
D.S.
be my song.
4.
Fm Ab/Bb Eb
Em G/A D
be my song.

## 63 I was lost but now I'm found

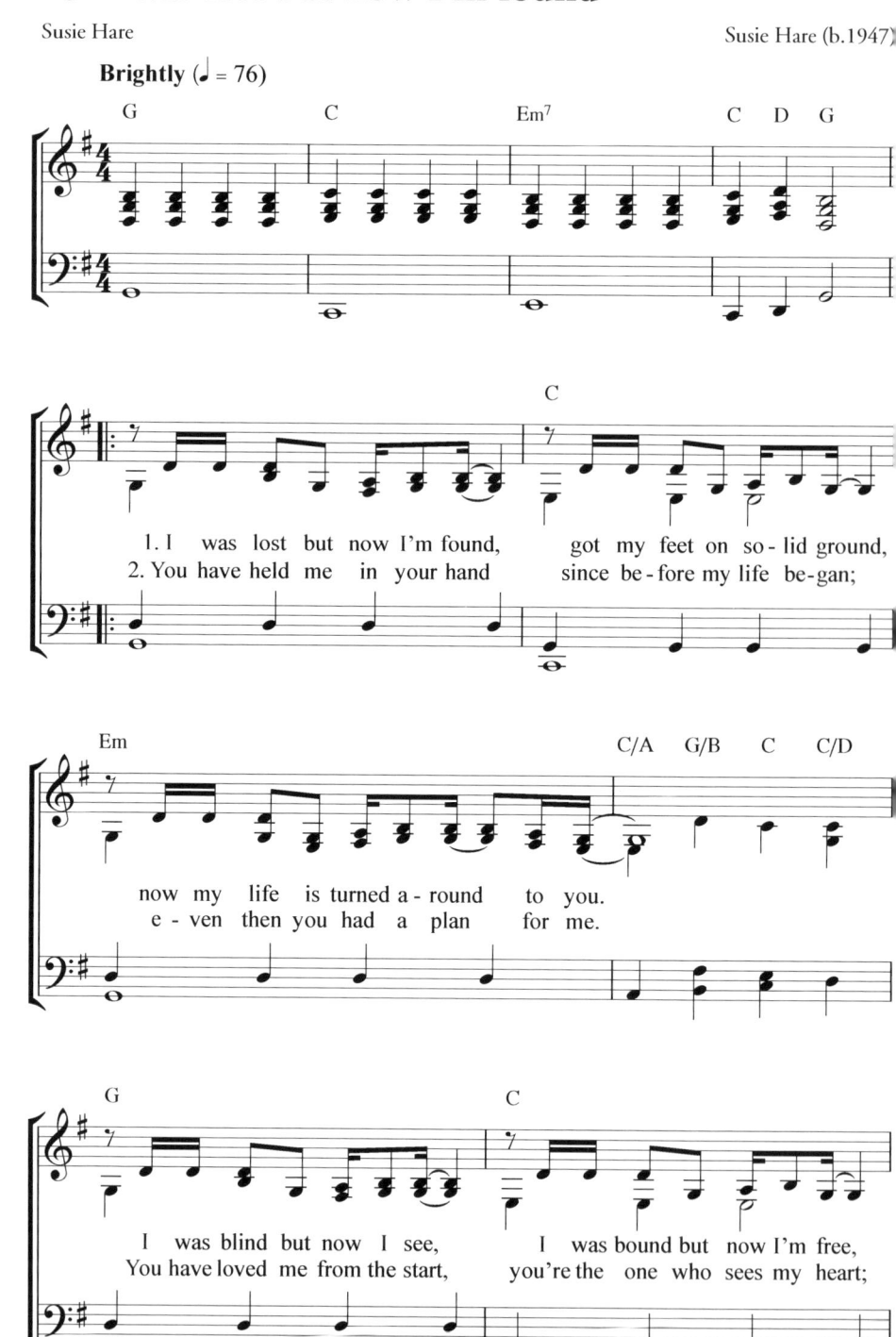

Susie Hare

Susie Hare (b.1947)

**Brightly** (♩ = 76)

1. I was lost but now I'm found, got my feet on solid ground,
2. You have held me in your hand since before my life began;

now my life is turned around to you.
even then you had a plan for me.

I was blind but now I see, I was bound but now I'm free,
You have loved me from the start, you're the one who sees my heart;

© Copyright 2015 Kevin Mayhew Ltd.
*It is illegal to photocopy music.*

and my life is set to be turned a-round to you.
now I'm gi-ving ev-'ry part, all of it to you.

*Refrain*
All that I have, all that I do, I give ev-'ry-thing to you. All that I am, all that I'll be, Je-sus, do your work in me. Je-sus, do your work in me,

make me what you want to see, ev-'ry-thing that I should be.

Je-sus, do your work in me, break-ing me and melt-ing me,

mould-ing me and fill-ing me; Je-sus do your work in me.

All that I have,

all that I do, I give ev-'ry-

D G
thing to you. All that I have,
C Em C D G
all that I do, I give ev - 'ry - thing to you.
G/B C
I was lost but now I'm found, got my feet on so - lid ground,
Em/B C D G
rit.
now my life is turned a - round, turned a - round to you.

## 64 I will always sing the praises

Susie Hare

Susie Hare (b.1947)

QUINTON 87 87 D

1. I will always sing the praises of the one who died for me, when he left his home in glory, for the cross of Calvary; when he brought the love of heaven for all the world to see. I will

© Copyright 2015 Kevin Mayhew Ltd.
*It is illegal to photocopy music.*

2. I will sing of the creator
   who gave my life its plan,
   of the one who even loved me
   long before my life began;
   of the one who knew my future
   and all that I would be.
   I will always sing the praises
   of the one who died for me.

3. I was lost but Jesus found me,
   put me back on solid ground,
   where my blinded eyes were opened
   and my life was turned around.
   Now I stand complete in Jesus
   and in his security.
   I will always sing the praises
   of the one who died for me.

4. I was stumbling in the darkness,
   where the fears kept flooding in;
   and my guilty heart was heavy
   with the greatness of my sin.
   But his love was even greater,
   his forgiveness set me free.
   I will always sing the praises
   of the one who died for me.

# 65 If we have never sought

*Jesus of the scars*

Garth Hewitt

Garth Hewitt

(♩ = 115)

we have ne - ver sought, we seek you now;
hea - vens frigh - ten us; they are too calm;

your eyes burn through the dark, our on - ly stars;
in all the u - ni - verse we have no place.

we must have sight of thorn - marks on your brow,
Our wounds are hurt - ing us; where is the balm?

© Copyright 2012 Kevin Mayhew Ltd.
*It is illegal to photocopy music.*

we must have you, O Jesus of the scars.
Lord Jesus, by your scars, we know your grace.

*Refrain*

2. The O

Jesus of the scars, we seek you now, O

Jesus of the scars, we seek you now. We

must have sight of thorn-marks on your brow, we

must have you, O Jesus of the scars.

3. The other gods were strong, but you were weak;
they rode, but you did stumble to a throne;
but to our wounds only God's wounds can speak,
and not a god has wounds, but you a-

lone. O Jesus of the scars, we seek you now,

O Jesus of the scars, we seek you now.

We must have sight of thorn-marks on your brow,

we must have you, O Jesus of the scars.

# Songs *for a* SERVANT CHURCH

# 66 Image of our God and Father

Edwin Le Grice (1911-1992)  
alt. The Editors

Malcolm Archer (b.1952)

HEAVENLY SPLENDOUR 87 87

1. Image of our God and Father, ruling all created things,
holding distant worlds together, Lord of glory, King of kings.

2. Stepping down from heav'nly splendour,
   taking here the lowest seat,
   by your humble birth among us
   washing your creation's feet:

3. By the towel, the bowl, the water,
   by the thorns, the nails, the spear:
   Lord have mercy, Christ have mercy,
   Love unknown, enfold us here!

This version of text © Copyright 2014, and music  
© Copyright 1992 Kevin Mayhew Ltd.  
*It is illegal to photocopy music.*

# 67 In an age of twisted values

Martin E. Leckebusch (b.1962)

Edward Elgar (1857-1934)
arr. Donald Thomson

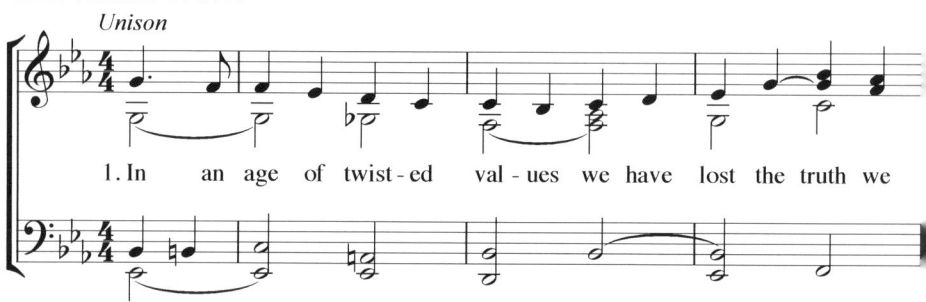

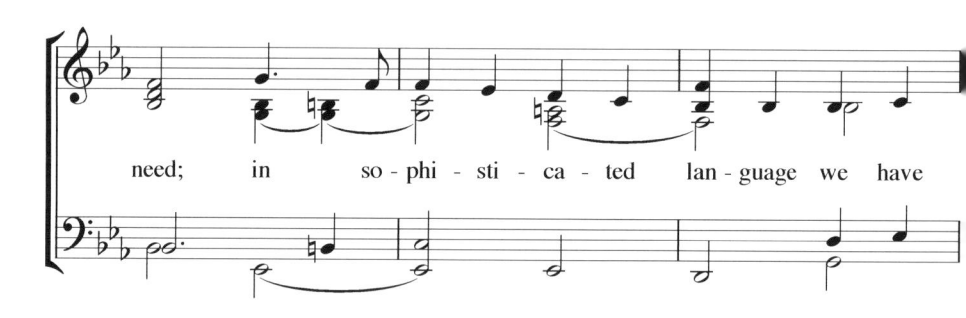

AVE VERUM 87 87 D

1. In an age of twist-ed val-ues we have lost the truth we need; in so-phi-sti-ca-ted lan-guage we have jus-ti-fied our greed; by our strug-gle for pos-ses-sions we have robbed the poor and weak — hear our cry and heal our

Text © Copyright 1999, and this music arrangement
© Copyright 2014 Kevin Mayhew Ltd.
*It is illegal to photocopy music.*

na - tion: your for - give - ness, Lord, we seek.

2. We have built discrimination
   on our prejudice and fear;
   hatred swiftly turns to cruelty
   if we hold resentments dear.
   For communities divided
   by the walls of class and race
   hear our cry and heal our nation:
   show us, Lord, your love and grace.

3. When our families are broken;
   when our homes are full of strife;
   when our children are bewildered,
   when they lose their way in life;
   when we fail to give the aged
   all the care we know we should —
   hear our cry and heal our nation
   with your tender fatherhood.

4. We who hear your word so often
   choose so rarely to obey;
   turn us from our wilful blindness,
   give us truth to light our way.
   In the power of your Spirit
   come to cleanse us, make us new:
   hear our cry and heal our nation
   till our nation honours you.

# 68 In glad and sad remembrance

Michael Forster (b.1946)　　　　　　　　　　　　　　　　　Gustav Holst (1874-1934)

THAXTED 13 13 13 13 13 13

1. In glad and sad re-mem-brance we ga-ther to re-call the lives, in all their full-ness that made and changed us all: the hopes and dis-ap-point-ments, the sor-row and the joy, the laugh-ter-la-den mem'ries that death could not des-troy; the

Text © Copyright 2004 Kevin Mayhew Ltd.
*It is illegal to photocopy music.*

love that touched and held us, the faith that set us free, the hope that still inspires us to be what we might be.

2. We join in recognising the common need we share
   to value and be valued, receive and offer care;
   to sing for joy and sorrow, to celebrate and grieve,
   to nurture and be nurtured, to give and to receive.
   So hope perfects within us her holy human sign,
   to each in each revealing the face of love divine.

3. Let this be our commitment to those we honour here:
   a vision of creation set free from pain and fear.
   We bear the gifts they gave us beyond this time and space,
   so ev'ry chance encounter becomes a work of grace;
   from eye to eye, from hand to hand, from soul to searching soul,
   love dances through our griefs and joys to make creation whole.

*Songs for a*
SERVANT
CHURCH

# 69 In the night, the sound of crying

Martin E. Leckebusch (b.1962)

Traditional English melody adapt. by
Ralph Vaughan Williams (1872-1958)

SUSSEX 87 87

1. In the night, the sound of crying — whimpers from a babe so small: angels hail the new-born infant in that dingy cattle-stall.

2. In the night, the sound of crying —
Mary journeys on with tears,
further from the home she treasures,
onward to uncertain years.

3. In the night, the sound of crying —
fury nothing can assuage!
Schemes of pointless, brutal murder
spring from Herod's jealous rage.

4. In the night, the sound of crying —
agonies beyond belief!
Soldiers searching, children slaughtered —
parents overwhelmed with grief.

5. In the night, the sound of crying —
cries of faith, though hope looks vain;
cries of joy, for Christ has conquered,
and, with justice, comes to reign.

Text © Copyright 2000 Kevin Mayhew Ltd.
Music © from 'The English Hymnal'. Reproduced by permission of Oxford University Press.
All rights reserved.
*It is illegal to photocopy music.*

# 70 In the peace of a garden

Nick Fawcett (b.1957)

Henry R. Bishop (1786-1855)
arr. Donald Thomson

HOME SWEET HOME 76 76 D

1. In the peace of a garden God gives the gift of life. Yet in o-pen re-bel-lion we take the way of strife. Our pa-ra-dise is for-feit, cre-a-tion groans in pain. Yet, gra-cious-ly, God pled-ges that life will bloom a-gain.

Text and this music arrangement
© Copyright 2014 Kevin Mayhew Ltd.
It is illegal to photocopy music.

2. In the peace of a garden
   our Saviour bows his head.
   On the cross he must suffer;
   tomorrow he'll be dead.
   His friends will soon deny him,
   abandon and betray,
   yet still his love continues;
   he knows no other way.

3. In the peace of a garden
   the night has turned to day;
   where they looked for his body
   the stone is rolled away.
   The broken Christ is risen —
   the one who'd cruelly died.
   He goes ahead before them,
   and walks now by their side.

4. In the peace of a garden
   the tree of life stands tall,
   as the Lamb greets his people,
   his grace renewing all.
   The enemy is broken;
   here waits our loving Lord!
   Our gracious God has spoken;
   our Eden is restored.

# 71 In vast, ornate cathedrals

Jean Holloway (b.1939)

From a melody in Johann Crüger's 'Gesangbuch' adapt. by William Henry Monk (1823-1889)

CRÜGER 76 76 D

1. In vast, ornate cathedrals of solid oak and stone, the Lord in all his greatness and majesty, is known; in humble rooms and kitchens he shares our daily meal; wherever bread is broken, Christ comes to bless and heal.

Text © Copyright 2000 Kevin Mayhew Ltd.
*It is illegal to photocopy music.*

2. Our vestments, in their splendour,
   the silver and the gold,
   make pageantry of worship,
   give richness to behold;
   our Saviour, in his lifetime,
   wore robes of common thread;
   a common cup and basket
   sufficed for wine and bread.

3. The liturgy we follow
   is high or broad or low,
   but through each form of worship,
   one Lord we come to know;
   Christ speaks through ev'ry language,
   in ev'ry time and place;
   he lives in diverse cultures,
   embraces ev'ry race.

4. Christ made his home with strangers,
   ignoring wealth and class;
   there was no social stigma
   his love could not surpass.
   He bore no rank or title,
   but came of lowly birth;
   he was both priest and outcast
   the years he walked the earth.

5. The Saviour of the broken
   restores and makes us whole;
   his presence reassures us,
   his tears and love console.
   No person is unworthy,
   he keeps no one apart;
   he waits in love and patience
   to enter ev'ry heart.

# 72 Is the church a building?

Lucy Berry (b.1957)                                            Michael Brierley (b.1932)

CAMBERWELL 65 65 D

1. Is the church a building? Is this church our own?
Is it made of people? Is it made of stone?
Is it shaped for welcome? Is it shaped for pray'r?
Is it for our comfort, or for our des-

Text © Copyright 2014 Kevin Mayhew Ltd.
Music © Copyright 1960 Josef Weinberger Ltd., 12-14 Mortimer Street, London W1T 3JJ. Used by permission.
*It is illegal to photocopy music.*

2. Is this church for strangers?
   Is this church for friends?
   Is it for a promise:
   life that never ends?
   Can this church be human?
   Can it be divine?
   Is it for all people,
   or is it just mine?

3. Is the church for mission?
   Is the church for peace?
   Is the church for action,
   or for our release?
   Is the church a promise?
   Is the church a place?
   Is the church for meeting
   you, Christ, face to face?

4. Thank you for the questions
   which this church must pose
   at our life's beginning,
   now, and at its close.
   Build us up, Christ Jesus,
   mind and strength and heart;
   so we learn to finish
   what we yearn to start.

# 73 It's the morning after

Barbara Glasson

Rod Boucher
arr. Marian Hellen

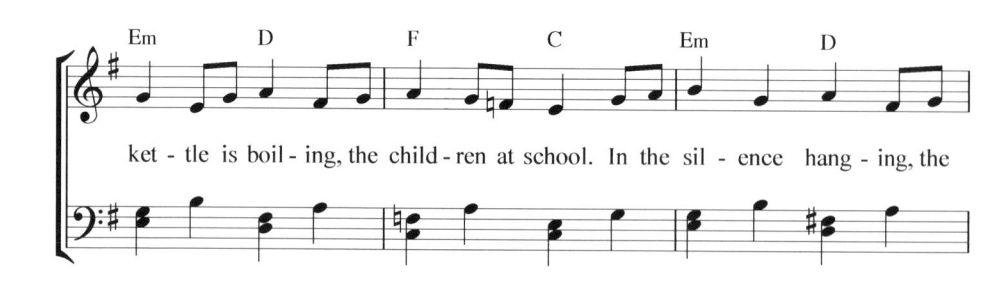

**Heartfelt and gentle**

1. It's the morn-ing af-ter the late night quar-rel, the ket-tle is boil-ing, the child-ren at school. In the sil-ence hang-ing, the

© Copyright 2015 Kevin Mayhew Ltd.
*It is illegal to photocopy music.*

trust that was bro-ken, a home be-yond con-flict but not yet at peace.

2. It's the morning after the right-wing rally,
   the streets have been swept and the banners are down.
   In the silence hanging, the pain that was shouted,
   a town beyond conflict but not yet at peace.

3. It's the morning after the signing of treaties,
   the flags have been raised for autonomous rule.
   In the silence hanging, the echoes of bombing,
   a land beyond conflict but not yet at peace.

4. It's the morning after the last good intention,
   yesterday's ruin, tomorrow's fresh start.
   In the silence hanging, the stories unspoken,
   a world beyond conflict but not yet at peace.

# 74 Jesus, in your life we see you

Basil E. Bridge (b.1927)        William Penfro Rowlands (1860-1937)

BLAENWERN 87 87 D

1. Jesus, in your life we see you making God's compassion known, 'Surely you have borne our sorrows, surely made our pain your own!' see your touch bring hope and healing, see your

Text © Copyright 1999 Kevin Mayhew Ltd.
*It is illegal to photocopy music.*

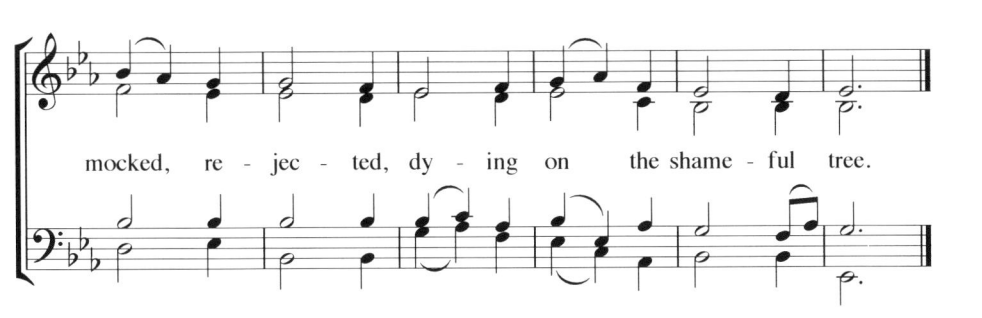

... word set cap-tives free, see you suf-fer, mocked, re-jec-ted, dy-ing on the shame-ful tree.

2. Risen Lord, you reign in glory;
but your wounds and scars remain;
you can share the outcast's suff'ring,
sound the depths of human pain,
know where greed exploits the helpless,
hear the addict's lonely cry,
grieve at so much waste and heartbreak,
feel for all who question 'why?'

3. Risen Lord, you bear their sorrow,
know how much they need your peace;
as you once healed broken bodies,
offered captive souls release,
take us, use us in your service;
we would follow where you lead;
only your divine compassion
meets the depths of human need.

## 75 Jesus meets us at the margins

Michael Forster (b.1946)                                                  Charles Crozat Converse (1832-1918)

WHAT A FRIEND (CONVERSE) 87 87 D

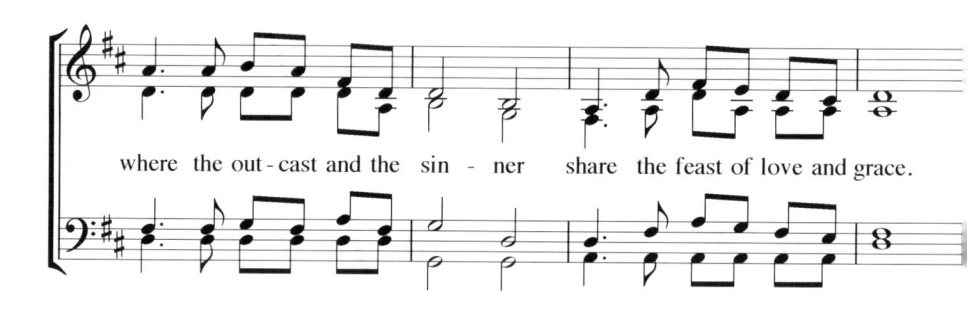

1. Jesus meets us at the margins;
calls us in to take our place
where the outcast and the sinner
share the feast of love and grace.
At the gates of ev-'ry city,
people whom the world rejects
find in this divine encounter
healing, honour and respect.

*Text © Copyright 1992 Kevin Mayhew Ltd.*
*It is illegal to photocopy music.*

2. Life in all its rich abundance
   Jesus freely offers here;
   see him make the wine of wholeness
   from the water of our fear!
   Jesus calls us to the margins,
   through the voice of those who wait:
   'All of you who share my kingdom,
   come and meet me at the gate.'

3. See him there in pain and sorrow,
   bearing still his people's sin;
   see him captive, cold and hungry,
   set him free and bring him in.
   Hear the royal invitation
   spoken to the last and least:
   'Come, you blessed of my Father,
   join me in the kingdom's feast!'

# 76 Jesus shall reign, his power be shown

Susie Hare

Susie Hare (b.1947)

FARRINGDON LM

Steadily  Capo 3

1. Jesus shall reign, his pow'r be shown, his greatness ev-'ry-where be known, and by his love, from shore to shore, lives will be changed to sin no more. Let all the world its praises bring, let ev-'ry voice its praises sing, until all hearts to him belong and all the

© Copyright 2015 Kevin Mayhew Ltd.
*It is illegal to photocopy music.*

2. Jesus shall reign, people will come
   in thankfulness for what he's done.
   The young and old from ev'ry land,
   before his throne will humbly stand.

3. Jesus shall reign, the world will see
   his pow'r displayed in victory.
   And Satan's curse will then be gone,
   extinguished by the mighty one.

# 77 Jesus, the Holy One

Susie Hare            Susie Hare (b.1947)

**Unhurried**

1. Jesus, the Holy One, the precious gift of God's own Son. Jesus, the Holy One, we bow before you now. *Refrain* We bow down, we bow down, we bow down be-

© Copyright 2001 Kevin Mayhew Ltd.
*It is illegal to photocopy music.*

2. Jesus, the Holy Lamb,
   the sacrifice of God for man.
   Jesus, the Holy Lamb,
   we bow before you now.

3. Jesus, the holy name
   that takes our sin, that bears our shame.
   Jesus, the holy name,
   we bow before you now.

# 78 Jesus, we have heard your Spirit    Where you lead us

Martin E. Leckebusch (b.1962)                              Susie Hare (b.1947)

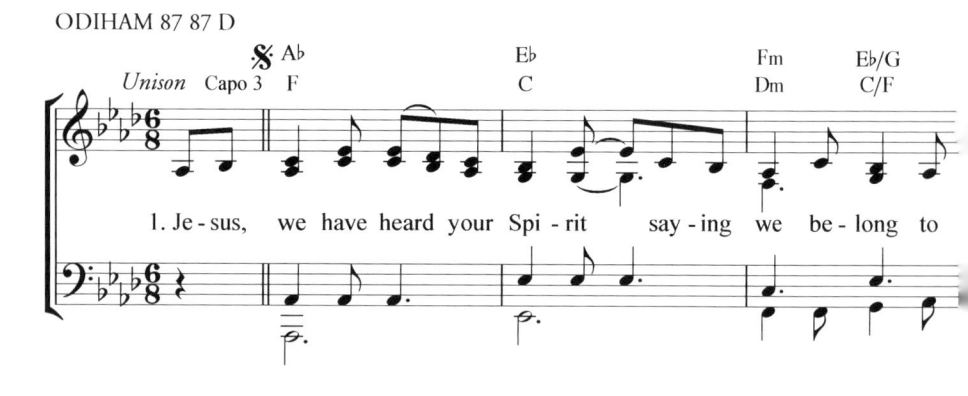

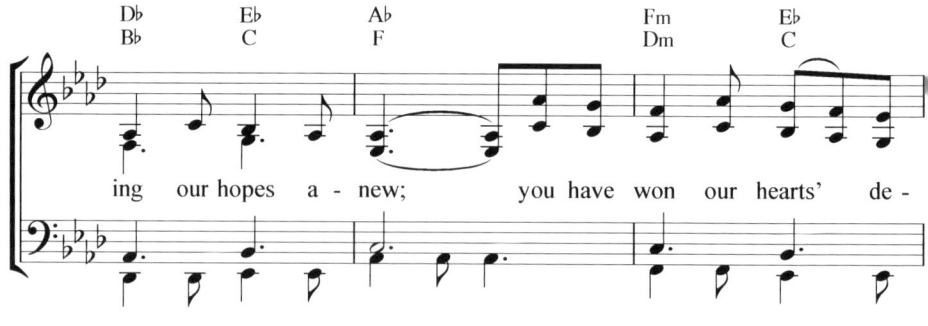

ODIHAM 87 87 D

1. Jesus, we have heard your Spirit saying we belong to you, showing us our need for mercy, focusing our hopes anew; you have won our hearts' devotion, now we feel your guiding hand: where you

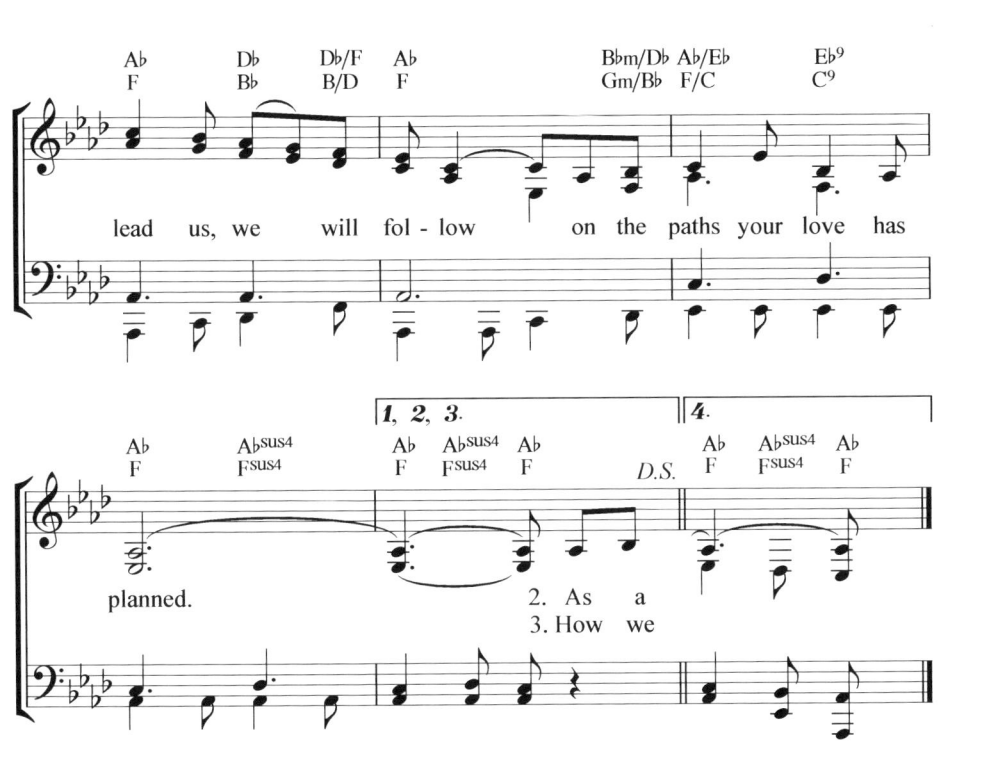

lead us, we will fol-low on the paths your love has planned.

2. As a
3. How we

2. As a chosen, pilgrim people
   we are learning day by day
   what it means to be disciples,
   to believe and to obey.
   Word and table show your purpose;
   hearts and lives we gladly bring –
   where you lead us, we will follow,
   suff'ring Saviour, risen King.

3. How we learn that ev'ry nation
   should exalt your matchless name,
   yet so often this world's systems
   contradict your regal claim.
   If we stand for truth and justice
   we, like you, may suffer loss;
   where you lead us, we will follow –
   give us grace to bear our cross.

4. So we journey on together,
   keen to make our calling sure:
   through our joys, our fears, our crises,
   may our faith be made mature.
   Jesus, hope of hearts and nations,
   sov'reign Lord of time and space,
   where you lead us, we will follow
   till we see you face to face.

# 79 Justice like a river

Garth Hewitt  
Garth Hewitt

(♩ = 75)

1. Jus-tice like a ri-ver, let it flow, let it flow.
2. Mer-cy flow-ing strong-ly, let it flow, let it flow.

Good news for the poor, let it flow, let it flow.
Heal-ing love and peace, let it flow, let it flow.

*Last time to Coda*

Like a ne-ver-fail-ing stream of jus-tice and of peace;
Strength for all the strug-gles, dig-ni-ty for all;

*Refrain*

jus-tice like a ri-ver, let it flow, let it flow. Let's u-nite
jus-tice like a ri-ver, let it flow, let it flow.

© Copyright 2012 Kevin Mayhew Ltd.  
*It is illegal to photocopy music.*

F G C Dm
un-der one tree, un - der the bran - ches of the
G F G C
o-live tree. Let's u-nite un-der one tree, un - der the sha-
Last time, repeat v.1
then to Coda
Dm C
- dow of the tree of life.
CODA
C G7 C
jus-tice like a ri-ver, let it flow, let it flow,
C G7 C
jus-tice like a ri-ver, let it flow, let it flow.

# 80 Let all creation's wonders

Martin E. Leckebusch (b.1962)  
John Richardson (1816-1879)

VAUGHAN 76 76 76 D

1. Let all creation's wonders and countless angel hordes unite in ceaseless worship to praise the Lord of lords: he spoke, and formed the cosmos; he set the stars in place; his voice defines the contours of interstellar space —  let

Text © Copyright 2001 Kevin Mayhew Ltd.  
*It is illegal to photocopy music.*

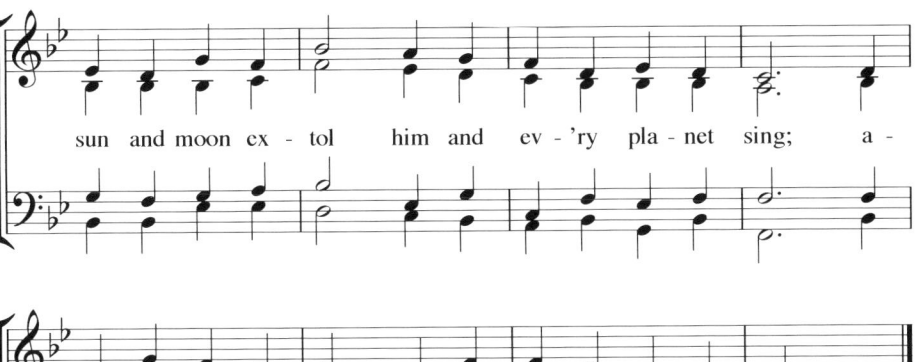

sun and moon extol him and ev-'ry planet sing; across the constellations let alleluias ring.

2. From far beneath the oceans
   let joyful songs arise,
   while hail and wind and lightning
   toss psalms across the skies.
   You beasts of farm and jungle,
   let nature's hymn be heard;
   tell out your maker's greatness,
   each insect, ev'ry bird;
   you peoples and you rulers,
   acknowledge him as King —
   from ev'ry generation
   let alleluias ring.

3. So let us lift our voices
   for all that we are worth
   to God whose timeless splendour
   surpasses heav'n and earth:
   in love he chose and called us,
   a people of his own,
   and gave to us a Saviour
   to make his mercy known.
   His name alone we honour;
   our lifelong praise we bring;
   from deep within our spirits
   let alleluias ring!

# 81 Let love be our glory

Michael Forster (b.1946)

James James (1833-1902)
arr. Donald Thomson

LAND OF MY FATHERS 11 11 11 8 and Refrain

1. Let love be our glory, our strength and our song, in face of injustice, courageous and strong, that labours with hope in the pains of the earth to bring peace and wholeness to birth.

Text and this music arrangement © Copyright 2014 Kevin Mayhew Ltd.
*It is illegal to photocopy music.*

*Refrain*

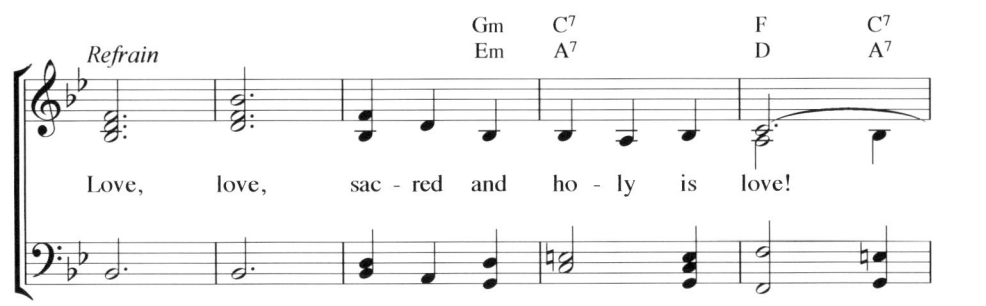

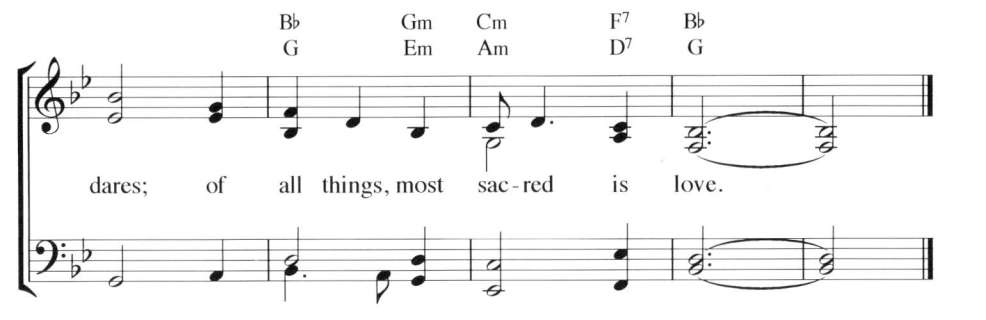

Love, love, sacred and holy is love!

Love holds, love shares; love dreams, love dares; of all things, most sacred is love.

2. The love that embraces, and yet lets us be,
the love beyond price, yet abundant and free,
that wounds us and heals us, that calls us and sends
our source and our ultimate end.

3. Let love, then, create in this time and this space,
for all who will enter, a haven of grace,
where all shall be welcome and all shall be free,
a place to become and to be.

## 82 Let love be real

Michael Forster (b.1946)                           Christopher Tambling (1964-2015)

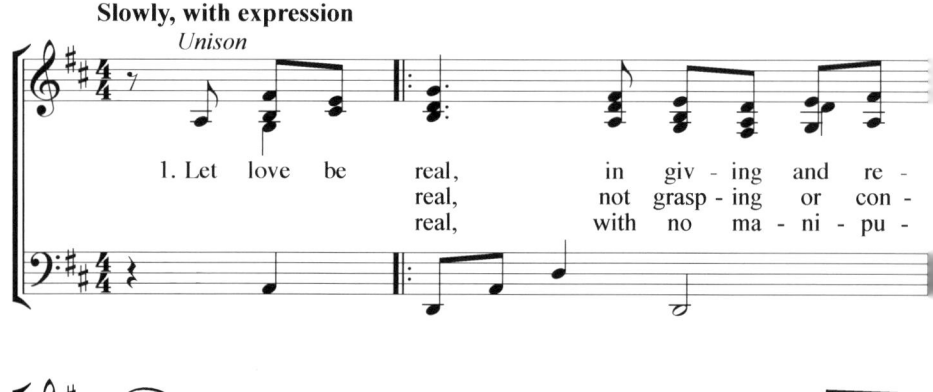

**Slowly, with expression**

1. Let love be real, in giving and receiving, without the need to manage and to own; a haven, free from posing and pretending where ev-'ry weakness may be safely tending

real, not grasping or conniving, that strange embrace that holds, yet sets us free; that helps us face the risk of truly living, and makes us brave to be what we might be

real, with no manipulation, no secret wish to harness and control. Let us accept each other's incompleteness, and share the joy of learning to be

© Copyright 1995 Kevin Mayhew Ltd.
*It is illegal to photocopy music.*

known. Give me your hand, a - long the des - ert
be. Give me your strength when all my words are
whole. Give me your hope, through dreams and dis - ap-

path - way, give me your love wher - e - ver we may
weak - ness, give me your love in spite of all you
point - ments; give me your trust when all my fail - ings

go.
know. As God loves us, so let us love each
show.

o - ther: with no de - mands, just o - pen hands and space to

*To next verse* | *Last time*

grow. 2. Let love be
3. Let love be grow.

# 83 Let the world be changed

Garth Hewitt                                                                                                   Garth Hewitt

(♩ = 100)

*Refrain*

Let the world be changed, let the rules be changed, let there be a place for ev-'ry-one.

*(Fine)*

© Copyright 2012 Kevin Mayhew Ltd.
*It is illegal to photocopy music.*

C
Dm7
Bring God's king-dom near, let all be wel - come here,
G7sus4
G
and may there be for all a just share.
C
Fsus2 F Gsus4 Em7
Fsus2 F
1. The scales of world
G G/B C Am Am/C
trade are un-bal-anced and un-fair be-tween
Dm7 G
the rich world and the poor.

Let faith re-store hope that the rules can be changed so bring-ing a just share to all.

2. Let's break bread together in a broken world,
   let's share the bread and together make a vow
   that the poor of the world, wherever they may be,
   may come and join the world's table now.

3. There are tariffs that keep the rich world rich
   and patents that keep the poor world out.
   If we sow injustice, we'll reap calamity;
   it's time to change the trade rules now.

# 84 Let us all, with grateful minds

Lucy Berry (b.1957)

From 'Hymn Tunes of the United Brethren'
adapt. by John Bernard Wilkes (1785-1869)

MONKLAND 77 and Refrain

1. Let us all, with grateful minds praise you, Lord, for being kind;

*Refrain*

all your mercies still endure; ever faithful, ever sure.

2. Even though our love is small,
   yet you love us one and all;

3. Even though the Word you speak
   goes unheeded week by week;

4. Even though we fail to do
   basic things you ask us to;

5. Even though we love to do
   things which hurt us and hurt you;

6. Help us learn that to forgive
   is your loving way to live;

7. Let us all with grateful minds
   praise you, Lord, for being kind;

Text © Copyright 2014 Kevin Mayhew Ltd.
*It is illegal to photocopy music.*

# 85 Let us rejoice

Martin E. Leckebusch (b.1962)        Malcolm Archer (b.1952)

STOGURSEY 10 10 10 and Alleluias

1. Let us rejoice: God's gift to us is peace! Here is the calm which bids our strivings cease, for God's acceptance brings a true release: alleluia, alleluia!

Text © Copyright 2001 Kevin Mayhew Ltd.
Music © Copyright Malcolm Archer.
*It is illegal to photocopy music.*

2. We can be strong, for now we stand by grace,
   held in his loving, fatherly embrace;
   his care remains, whatever trials we face:
   alleluia, alleluia!

3. We trust in God, and shall not be dismayed,
   nor find our hopes of glory are betrayed,
   for all his splendour we shall see displayed:
   alleluia, alleluia!

4. And come what may, we never need despair —
   God is at work through all the griefs we bear,
   that in the end his likeness we may share:
   alleluia, alleluia!

5. Deep in our hearts the love of God is found;
   his precious gifts of life and joy abound —
   so let our finest songs of praise resound:
   alleluia, alleluia!

# Songs
## *for a*
## SERVANT
## CHURCH

# 86 Light of her life

Nick Fawcett (b.1957)

Thomas Dekker (c.1572-1632)
arr. Donald Thomson

GOLDEN SLUMBERS LM

**Gently**

1. Light of her life, meets Mary's gaze;
burst-ing with pride she of-fers praise.
God's spe-cial gift, source of such joy —
there in the straw, her pre-cious boy.

2. Light in the fields floods from the sky;
angels announce news from on high.
Shepherds amazed, hurriedly run —
there in the hay, God's only Son.

3. Light of a star, leading the way,
calling for faith, wise men obey.
Gifts of great price, humbly they bring,
meant for a child, fit for a king.

4. Light of the world sent from above,
sharing such peace, showing such love.
Coming to bless, coming to save —
there at the tomb life from the grave.

5. Light for my path filling my soul,
reaching within, making me whole.
Jesus is born, lift up your voice!
With all our hearts, let us rejoice!

Text and this music arrangement
© Copyright 2014 Kevin Mayhew Ltd.
*It is illegal to photocopy music.*

# 87 Listen up

Barbara Glasson

Rod Boucher
arr. Marian Hellen

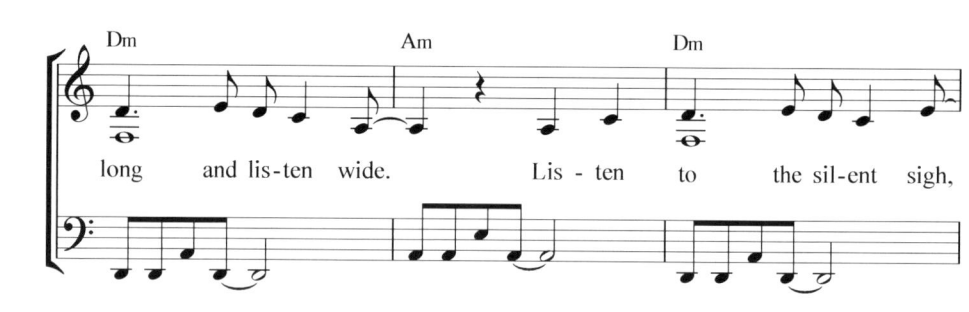

**With thoughtful joy**

1. Lis-ten up and lis-ten out, lis-ten long and lis-ten wide. Lis-ten to the sil-ent sigh, lis-ten to the noi-sy cry.

© Copyright 2015 Kevin Mayhew Ltd.
*It is illegal to photocopy music.*

2. Listen up and listen in,
   listen deep and listen round.
   Listen to the deepest doubt,
   listen to the loudest sound.

3. Listen up and listen late,
   listen wide and listen long.
   Listen to the voiceless song,
   listen to the truth inside.

4. Listen up and listen high,
   listen round and listen out.
   Listen past the shouted hate,
   listen to the joyful shout!

# 88 Living God, your word has called us

Jan Berry  Malcolm Archer (b.1952)

TOR HILL 87 87 D

1. Living God, your word has called us, summoned us to live by grace, make us one in hope and vision, as we gather in this place. Take our searching, take our praising, take the silence of our prayer, offered up in

© Copyright 1999 Kevin Mayhew Ltd.
*It is illegal to photocopy music.*

joy - ful wor-ship, spring - ing from the love we share.

2. Living God, your love has called us
in the name of Christ your Son,
forming us to be his body,
by your Spirit making one.
Working, laughing, learning, growing,
old and young and black and white,
gifts and skills together sharing,
in your service all unite.

3. Living God, your hope has called us
to the world that you have made,
teaching us to live for others,
humble, joyful, unafraid.
Give us eyes to see your presence,
joy in laughter, hope in pain.
In our loving, in our living,
give us strength that Christ may reign.

# 89 Living water

Barbara Glasson

Rod Boucher
arr. Marian Hellen

**Very gently**

1. In an at-tic, in a gar-age, in a late night show, he got high, she got low.

© Copyright 2015 Kevin Mayhew Ltd.
It is illegal to photocopy music.

2. In an alley, in a tantrum, in a drunken fit,
   he got tight, she got hit.
3. On the web, in the dark, not yet turned sixteen,
   he got caught, she got seen.
4. By a well, out of town, a bucketload of shame.
   He eased a thirst, she found her name.

# 90 Long ago you taught your people

Martin E. Leckebusch (b.1962)

Croatian folk melody adapt. by
Franz Joseph Haydn (1732-1809)

AUSTRIA 87 87 D

1. Long a-go you taught your peo-ple: 'Part of what you reap is mine — from your cat-tle, bring the first-born; tithe the crops of field and vine.' Though be-neath the law's re-stric-tions we are not com-pelled to live, as we reap our

Text © Copyright 2000 Kevin Mayhew Ltd.
*It is illegal to photocopy music.*

month-ly har-vest, make us ea-ger, Lord, to give.

2. What a way of life you showed us
through the Son you gladly gave:
never snared by earthly treasure,
buried in a borrowed grave —
yet to all he freely offered
riches of the deepest kind:
let us live with his example
firmly fixed in heart and mind.

3. In the lifestyle of the Spirit
giving has a central part;
teach us, Lord, this grace of sharing
with a cheerful, loving heart —
not a tiresome obligation,
not a barren legal due,
but an overflow of worship:
all we have belongs to you!

# 91 Lord, at a time when our tables are laden

Martin E. Leckebusch (b.1962)          Joseph Francis Thrupp (1827-1867)

EPIPHANY 11 10 11 10

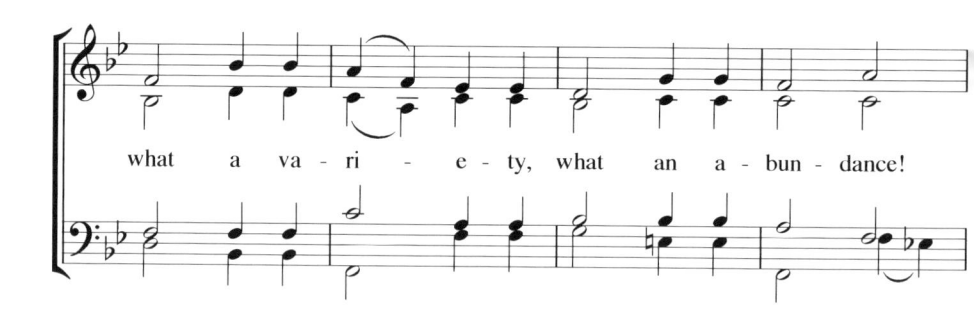

1. Lord, at a time when our tables are laden,
tasting your goodness, we bring you our praise:
what a variety, what an abundance!
Such is your faithfulness, crowning our days.

Text © Copyright 2009 Kevin Mayhew Ltd.
*It is illegal to photocopy music.*

2. Food for our nourishment, food for enjoyment,
   produce of labour and climate and land,
   brought by a network of markets and transport —
   all of it comes from the same gracious hand.

3. Kindle our thanks for the wealth of creation,
   orchards and fields you have lovingly blessed;
   keep us from squandering earth's good resources,
   hoarding the harvests and stealing the best.

4. Teach us to honour the work of our neighbours,
   paying a wage that is timely and fair;
   open our eyes and our hearts to the needy,
   making us mindful of all we can share.

5. Lord, shape our values, our toil and our trading;
   prompt us to live ev'ry day as we should,
   till all the world shares the feast of your kindness,
   tastes your abundance, and knows you are good.

# 92 Lord, change our world

Nick Fawcett (b.1957)

Maewa Kaihau, Clement Scott
and Dorothy Stewart
arr. Sarah Watts

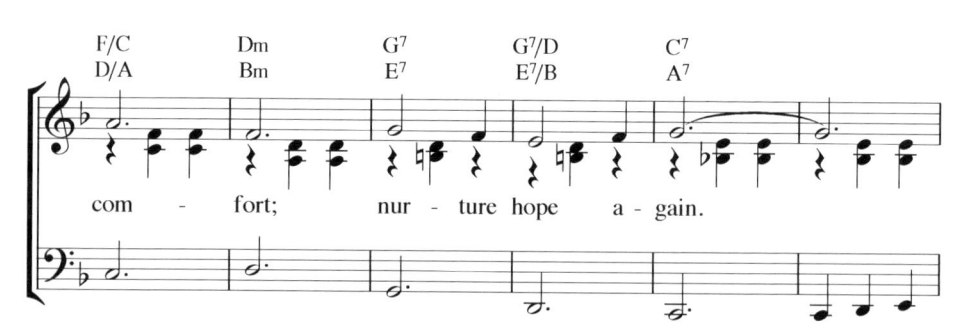

1. Lord, change our world — its suf-fer-ing and pain. Reach out to com-fort; nur-ture hope a-gain.

Text © Copyright 2014, and this music arrangement
© Copyright 2009 Kevin Mayhew Ltd.
*It is illegal to photocopy music.*

F D
Bb/D G/B
Bbm/Db Gm/Bb
F/C D/A
F D
C7 A7
Heal and re - vive; Lord, hear us we im -
F D
Bb G
Gm/Bb Em/G
F/C D/A
D7 B7
plore. Grant us your touch; re - fa - shion
To next verse
Last time
G7 E7
C7 A7
F D
F D
and re - store.
done.

2. Lord, change our world — its poverty and need.
   Reach out to challenge, minister and feed.
   Bless and provide; replenish and renew.
   Show us your love; display your word is true.

3. Lord, change our world — its bitterness and tears.
   Reach out and scatter darkness, grief and fears.
   Bind up our wounds; remind us that you care.
   Help us to know that always you are there.

4. Lord, change our world — its cruelty and hate.
   Reach out to rescue; save us from our fate.
   End war and strife, and help to make us one.
   Grant that your will shall finally be done.

## 93 Lord, give us vision

Jean Holloway (b.1939)     James William Elliot (1833-1915)

CHURCH TRIUMPHANT LM

1. Lord, give us vision new and clear of what the future church can be; we seek to build foundations here for one diverse community.

2. O Saviour, teach us how to live
without division, hurt or wrong;
the gift to heal, you freely give,
to make your people whole and strong.

3. O faithful Spirit, keep us true
to vows we made in Jesus' name;
help us to walk in faith with you,
and live the gospel we proclaim.

4. O Trinity, now send us out
inspired for mission once again;
sustain our hope, transcend our doubt,
to bring the world to Christ. Amen.

Text © Copyright 2000 Kevin Mayhew Ltd.
*It is illegal to photocopy music.*

# 94 Lord Jesus, plant a seed of faith

Martin E. Leckebusch (b.1962)  Kevin Mayhew (b.1942)

THORPE MORIEUX CM

1. Lord Jesus, plant a seed of faith
and let it grow in me,
to bear a harvest shown by deeds
of lasting quality.

2. Grant me a gentle, humble heart
where love alone holds sway,
till selfless servanthood becomes
my habit day by day.

3. Give me a deeper, richer hope,
a vision sure and clear,
to strengthen me until the day
when you at last appear.

4. I have no faith but what you give;
your love has made me new;
my hope is found in no one else —
Lord, give me more of you!

© Copyright 2013 Kevin Mayhew Ltd.
*It is illegal to photocopy music.*

# 95 Lord, today your voice is calling

Nick Fawcett (b.1957)      Susie Hare (b.1947)

MELFORD 87 87 D

1. Lord, to-day your voice is call-ing, lift-ing thoughts to things a-bove; life is won-der-ful, en-thrall-ing, touched by your un-fail-ing love. Sud-den-ly I see the beau-ty of-ten hid-den from my gaze, so I come, not

\* These guitar chords should be played only with the melody, to give a Music Group arrangement.

© Copyright 2004 Kevin Mayhew Ltd.
*It is illegal to photocopy music.*

*...out of duty, but with glad and grateful praise.*

2. Lord, I sometimes fail to value
   all your blessing as I should.
   Slow to make the time to thank you,
   blind to so much that is good.
   Days are lived in such a hurry
   there's no time to stop and stare,
   joy is crushed by weight of worry,
   happiness obscured by care.

3. Lord, today I come rejoicing,
   vowed to waste your gifts no more;
   bringing praise and gladly voicing
   what I should have voiced before.
   Pouring out my adoration,
   scarcely knowing where to start,
   with a song of exultation,
   Lord, I thank you from the heart.

# 96 Lord, we know that we have failed you

Nick Fawcett (b.1957)             Noel Rawsthorne (b.1929)

WILLASTON 87 87 D

1. Lord, we know that we have failed you, false and foolish in so much, loath to listen to your guidance, slow to recognise your touch. Though we keep you at a distance, by our side, Lord, still remain; cleanse our hearts, re-

© Copyright 1999 Kevin Mayhew Ltd.
*It is illegal to photocopy music.*

new our spi - rits, give us grace to start a - gain.

2. Lord, we know that we have failed you,
through the things we do and say,
though we claim to care for others
we have thrust their needs away.
Too concerned with our own comfort
we have added to their pain;
teach us to show faith in action,
give us grace to start again.

3. Lord, we know that we have failed you,
too familiar with your word,
even though you've spoken clearly
all too often we've not heard.
Closed to truths which stretch horizons
or which go against the grain —
teach us, Lord, to stop and listen,
give us grace to start again.

4. Lord, we know that we have failed you,
lives too fraught to stop and stare;
dwelling always on the present —
what to eat or drink or wear.
Teach us first to seek your kingdom,
in our hearts for ever reign;
send us out, restored, forgiven,
give us grace to start again.

# 97 Lord, what a sacrifice I see

*The greatest love*

Susie Hare

Susie Hare (b.1947)

**Steadily**

1. Lord, what a sacrifice I see as I turn my eyes to Calvary; there, my sins nailed to a tree, a King stands in instead of me.
2. Lord, what a promise of your grace as I turn my eyes to seek your face; clothed in righteousness, I place my sinfulness in your embrace.
3. Lord, what a privilege I own to freely come before your throne; there, to know and to be known, surrendered now to you alone.

*Refrain*

© Copyright 2001 Kevin Mayhew Ltd.
*It is illegal to photocopy music.*

greatest love that I will ever know, the only love that never lets me go, streams from a heart that loves so perfectly; the greatest love of all is yours to me. me.

# 98 Lord, you amaze us

Nick Fawcett (b.1957)

Edward Elgar (1857-1934)
arr. Donald Thomson

**SALUT D'AMOUR 11 11 11 6**

1. Lord, you amaze us with your love and goodness,
bless us each day with life in all its fullness;
nothing in life or death shall come between us.
Great is your love, my God.

2. Lord, you immerse us in your peace and stillness;
   calming the storm within, you bring us quietness;
   nothing we used to dread shall come between us.
   Great is your peace, my God.

3. Lord, you astound us with your grace and kindness;
   false though we daily prove, you deem us faultless;
   nothing we do or say shall come between us.
   Great is your grace, my God.

4. Lord, I would give myself to you more nearly,
   serve you with all I am, with all you give me,
   show you, with heart and soul, I love you dearly.
   Great is your name, my God.

# 99 Lord, you have blessed me

Nick Fawcett (b.1957)　　　　　　　　　　　　　　　　　Kevin Mayhew (b.1942)

BUXHALL 10 10 10 10

1. Lord, you have blessed me and filled me with joy, grant-ing me life that no ill can de-stroy. Day af-ter day brings new rea-son to praise, bles-sings to thrill and de-lights to a-maze. heart.

*To next verse* / *Last time*

© Copyright 2013 Kevin Mayhew Ltd.
*It is illegal to photocopy music.*

2. Guidance, forgiveness, renewal and grace,
   strength and support in whatever I face,
   peace beyond words, constant help from above —
   so much each moment affirms your great love.

3. Morning by morning new mercies I see,
   gifts beyond number and all of them free.
   How can I thank you, Lord? Where can I start?
   Hear now my worship — it comes from the heart.

# Songs *for a* SERVANT CHURCH

# 100 Mary, blessèd teenage mother

Michael Forster (b.1946)                                                              Alan Ridout (1934-1996)

BLACK MADONNA 87 87 77

1. Mary, blessed teenage mother, with what holy joy you sing!
Humble, yet above all other, from your womb shall healing spring.
Out of wedlock pregnant found, full of grace with blessing crowned.

2. Mother of the homeless stranger
only outcasts recognise,
point us to the modern manger;
not a sight for gentle eyes!
Oh the joyful news we tell:
'Even here, Immanuel!'

3. Now, throughout the townships ringing,
hear the black madonna cry,
songs of hope and freedom singing,
poor and humble lifted high.
Here the Spirit finds a womb
for the breaker of the tomb!

4. Holy mother, for the nations
bring to birth the child divine:
Israel's strength and consolation,
and the hope of Palestine!
All creation reconciled
in the crying of a child!

© Copyright 1996 Kevin Mayhew Ltd.
*It is illegal to photocopy music.*

# 101 Mighty, magnificent God

Susie Hare  
Susie Hare (b.1947)

1, 2, 3. Mighty, magnificent God,

(1.) author of life, King of creation;  
(2.) all you have made speaks of your greatness.  
(3.) maker of all, Lord of all nations,

mountains and valleys rejoice,  
Once there was nothing at all;  
one day earth's people will come,

oceans resound in celebra-  
over the earth, all was in dark-  
bringing their praise, in adora-

© Copyright 2015 Kevin Mayhew Ltd.  
*It is illegal to photocopy music.*

A D/F♯ G A A7/G
- tion. The heav'ns de - clare your glo - ry, the
- ness. But in your sov-'reign pow - er and
- tion; ac - know - ledg - ing your glo - ry, the
D/F♯ G A D/F♯ G
earth sings out your praise, and nat - ure, in its beau -
at your word's com - mand, the whole earth was e - stab -
won - ders of your hand, un - til cre - a - tion's sto -
A A7/G D/F♯ G A
- ty, your han - di - work dis - plays.
- lished by your Cre - a - tor's hand.
- ry is heard in ev - 'ry land.
Refrain
D C G/B A
You are the po - wer that rules the sea,
Last time: You are the po - wer that rules the sea,

D C G/B A D C
you reign for e - ver in ma - jes - ty, you are the one who will
you are the love that em - bra - ces me; O, what a glo - ri - ous
G/B A Em7 D/F♯
al - ways be migh - ty, mag - ni - fi - cent God,
mys - te - ry: migh - ty, mag - ni - fi - cent God,
1, 2.
F G/A C
migh - ty, mag - ni - fi - cent God.
3.
F G/A C G/A C To Bridge
migh - ty, mag - ni - fi - cent God.
4.
G G/A D D/A D.S.
migh - ty, mag - ni - fi - cent God,

5.
G
poco rit.
G/A
D
Fine
migh - ty, mag - ni - fi - cent God.
Bridge
A
G/D
D
High a - bove all in your sov - 'reign - ty,
yet you reach down to hu - ma - ni - ty.
A
G/D
D
Em7
Lord of the earth and the sky and sea, of all that
O, how a - maz - ing that you should be a Fa - ther
1.
D/F♯
G
A
Bm/A
A
is and is to be;
2.
D/F♯
G
A
D.S.
and a Friend to me!

# Songs *for a* SERVANT CHURCH

# 102 Mother of Christ, called from above

Nick Fawcett (b.1957)                         Susie Hare (b.1947)

MOTHER OF CHRIST 88 10 10

1. Mother of Christ, called from above, chosen to serve,
chosen to love, freely you offered your body, your all,
no price too costly to answer God's call.

2. Mother of Christ, called from on high,
wondering how, wondering why;
yet you were willing to bow to God's will,
ready to serve him in good times or ill.

3. Mother of Christ, called from the crowd,
honoured by God, singing aloud,
gladly rejoicing, you poured out your praise,
heart overflowing and spirit ablaze.

4. Mother of Christ, called to respond,
bearing a child, gift from beyond.
Angels in splendour have gathered to sing.
Shepherds and magi revere him as king.

5. Mother of Christ, called here today,
we too would serve; guide us, we pray.
Speak to us, teach us — from you we would learn:
help us to honour the Saviour in turn.

© Copyright 2005 Kevin Mayhew Ltd.
*It is illegal to photocopy music.*

# 103 No gift so wonderful

## *Have we any room for Jesus?*

Susie Hare  
Susie Hare (b.1947)

**Unhurried**

1. No gift so won-der-ful, no love so beau-ti-ful, in just a hum-ble birth, heaven came down to earth. And in the still of night, the world was given light,

2. No gift so won-der-ful, no love so beau-ti-ful; what are we meant to see is it just history? And is he still, we find, a baby in our mind,

© Copyright 2001 Kevin Mayhew Ltd.  
*It is illegal to photocopy music.*

E♭add2 E♭ B♭/D Cm D♭
Dadd2 D A/C♯ Bm C
as in-to sin and shame, the love of hea-ven came.
and is the sta-ble scene all it will e-ver mean?
B♭sus4 B♭ E♭ E♭/D Cm Gm7 Csus4 C
Asus4 A D D/C♯ Bm F♯m7 Bsus4 B
Refrain
Have we a-ny time for Je-sus?
Have we a-ny room for Je-sus?
Fm7 B♭7 E♭maj7 Cm D♭m7♭5 Gsus4 G
Em7 A7 Dmaj7 Bm Cm7♭5 F♯sus4 F♯
Have we a-ny time to spare? If we turned our eyes, may-
Have we a-ny time for him? Are we on our own or
1. Cm Cm7 Fsus4 F B♭sus4 B♭7
Bm Bm7 Esus4 E Asus4 A7
be we'd re-cog-nise that he is there.
2. Cm Cm7 F7 Fm B♭ E♭
Bm Bm7 E7 Em A D
1st time D.C.
could we give a home to Christ the King?

# Songs *for a* SERVANT CHURCH

# 104 Now as the evening shadows fall

Michael Forster (b.1946)
based on 'Te lucis ante terminum'

Plainsong, accompaniment
by Andrew Moore (b.1954)

TE LUCIS LM

1. Now as the evening shadows fall, God our Creator, hear our call:
help us to trust your constant grace, though darkness seems to hide your face.

2. Help us to find, in sleep's release,
   bodily rest and inner peace;
   so may the darkness of the night
   refresh our eyes for morning light.

3. Father almighty, holy Son,
   Spirit eternal, three in One,
   grant us the faith that sets us free
   to praise you for eternity.

© Copyright 1999 Kevin Mayhew Ltd.
*It is illegal to photocopy music.*

# 105 Now, come to the water

Kevin Mayhew
based on Isaiah 55:1-4

Kevin Mayhew (b.1942)

FELSHAM 86 96 and Refrain

*Unison*

Now, come to the water, all you who are thirsty, and drink, drink deeply. Without terms or conditions, not a dress-code in sight, you'll be welcome to drink all you can.

1. Come,

© Copyright 1984, 2014 Kevin Mayhew Ltd.
*It is illegal to photocopy music.*

*take your choice of food and wine: ev-'ry-thing here is free! Why spend your money on worthless things: ev-'ry-thing here is free! Now,*

2. Now, listen well and you will find
   food that will feed your soul.
   Just come to me and receive your share,
   food that will feed your soul.

3. I promise you good things to come;
   you are my chosen ones.
   I name you witnesses to my world;
   you are my chosen ones.

# 106 Now is the time

Nick Fawcett (b.1957)

Maewa Kaihau, Clement Scott
and Dorothy Stewart
arr. Sarah Watts

1. Now is the time: a time to say good-bye. Soon he'll be hanging on a cross to die.

Text © Copyright 2014, and this music arrangement
© Copyright 2009 Kevin Mayhew Ltd.
*It is illegal to photocopy music.*

2. Now is the time: his end is drawing near.
   See how he trembles, racked with grief and fear.
   'Soon I must die,' he tells them; 'watch and pray.
   Give me the strength I need to face that day.'

3. Now is the time: his hour is nearly past.
   Soon he must suffer, soon will breathe his last.
   'Stay close to me,' he begs them; 'hear my call.
   Give me the strength I need to give my all.'

4. Now is the time: his work is nearly done.
   Soon he'll surrender life for ev'ryone.
   'Though all seems lost,' he tells us, 'don't despair.
   For, after death you'll find me waiting there.'

*Songs for a*
SERVANT
CHURCH

# 107 O Christ, remember them

Lucy Berry (b.1957)  Samuel Webbe (1740-1816)

MELCOMBE LM

1. O Christ, remember them: cut down by hate and pain in waste and war; torn from the ones they loved the most, in unmarked graves, who breathe no more.

2. O Christ, remember us: cut down
   by wounds of loss that will not heal,
   torn from the ones we loved the most,
   disabled by the grief we feel.

3. O Christ, remember us as yours
   worn as we are by raw regret
   and teach your limping, bleeding world
   to lean on you — and not forget.

Text © Copyright 2014 Kevin Mayhew Ltd.
*It is illegal to photocopy music.*

# 108 O Father, on your love we call

Jean Holloway (b.1939)        John Bacchus Dykes (1823-1876)

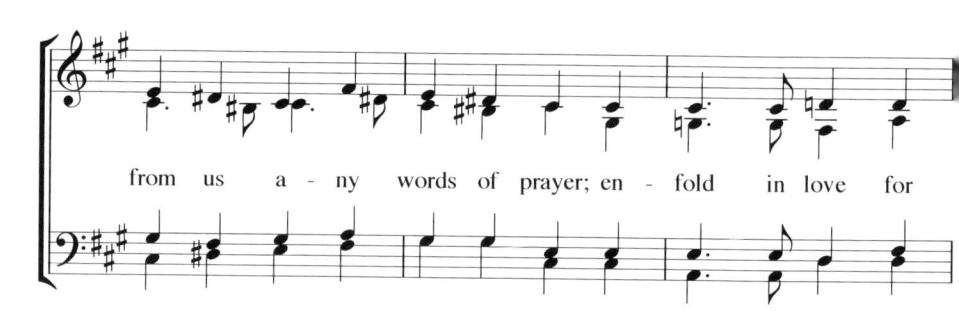

MELITA 88 88 88

1. O Father, on your love we call, when sorrow overshadows all, and pain that feels too great to bear drives from us any words of prayer; enfold in love for evermore the one we love, but see no more.

*Text © Copyright 2000 Kevin Mayhew Ltd.*
*It is illegal to photocopy music.*

2. Our child, so innocent and dear,
   was still untouched by guilt and fear;
   his *(her)* precious life had more to give,
   in him *(her)*, our hopes and dreams could live;
   enfold in love for evermore
   all those we love, but see no more.

3. So brief, the joy since he *(she)* was born,
   so long the years in which to mourn;
   give us compassion to sustain
   each other in this time of pain;
   enfold in love for evermore
   all those we love, but see no more.

4. Guard us from bitterness and hate,
   and share with us grief's crushing weight;
   help us to live from day to day,
   until, once more, we find our way;
   enfold in love for evermore
   all those we love, but see no more.

5. When friends assembled here must part,
   and dark despair invades the heart
   light one small flame of hope that still
   you walk with us, and always will;
   enfold in love for evermore
   all those we love, but see no more.

# Songs *for a* SERVANT CHURCH

## 109 O God of hope

Basil E. Bridge (b.1927)　　　　　　　　　Charles Hubert Hastings Parry (1848-1918)

REPTON 86 88 6

1. O God of hope, your prophets spoke of days when war would cease: when, taught to see each person's worth, and faithful stewards of the earth, we all would live in peace, we all would live in peace.

2. We pray that our divided world
   may hear their words anew:
   then lift for good the curse of war,
   let bread with justice bless the poor,
   and turn in hope to you,
   and turn in hope to you.

3. Earth's fragile web of life demands
   our rev'rence and our care,
   lest in our folly, sloth and greed,
   deaf both to you and others' need,
   we lay our planet bare,
   we lay our planet bare.

4. Earth's rich resources give us pow'r
   to build or to destroy:
   your Spirit urges us to turn
   from selfish, fear-bound ways, and learn
   his selfless trust and joy,
   his selfless trust and joy.

5. The Prince of Peace is calling us
   to shun the way of strife:
   he brings us healing through his pain;
   our shattered hope is born again
   through his victorious life,
   through his victorious life.

Text © Copyright 1999 Kevin Mayhew Ltd.
*It is illegal to photocopy music.*

## 110 O God of thoughts and feelings

Michael Forster (b.1946)          Samuel Sebastian Wesley (1810-1876)

AURELIA 76 76 D

1. O God of thoughts and feelings, of spirit and of mind, accept the fears and questions we cannot leave behind. You walked this earth before us, you knew its joy and pain, and from its darkest moments launched hope's eternal reign.

Text © Copyright 2014 Kevin Mayhew Ltd.
*It is illegal to photocopy music.*

2. We honour all those people
   who face, without pretence,
   their inner doubts and anger,
   and think them no offence;
   those deepest, darkest feelings,
   we hardly dare to own,
   true faith may freely offer,
   unvarnished, at your throne.

3. Oh for the faith and courage
   to find you such a friend,
   assured that in your presence
   our hearts need not pretend.
   When pray'r is met with silence,
   and wounds refuse to heal,
   give us the faith to trust you
   with how we truly feel.

4. We come with hope and sorrow,
   with gratitude and pain,
   as this great gift you gave us
   returns to you again.
   There, in your perfect presence,
   shall ev'ry wound be healed,
   all anger turned to wonder,
   and perfect truth revealed.

# 111 O holy, heavenly kingdom

Michael Forster (b.1946)        Henri Friedrich Hémy (1818-1888)

**TURRIS DAVIDICA 76 76 D**

1. O holy, heav'n-ly king-dom God's faith-ful long to see, where peace and whole-ness pros-per and ev-'ry heart is free, where jus-tice flows like foun-tains and prai-ses ne-ver cease, come, make your home a-mong us, and give this world your peace.

Text © Copyright 2004 Kevin Mayhew Ltd.
*It is illegal to photocopy music.*

2. Among us and around us,
   yet veiled from mortal sight,
   the vision of the prophets
   and God's proclaimed delight;
   where tears find consolation,
   and open wounds are healed,
   where eyes and ears are opened,
   the kingdom is revealed.

3. Oh call us to your table,
   invite us to the feast,
   where Christ will bring together
   the greatest and the least,
   where grace will flow among us
   like rich, abundant wine,
   and those the world rejected
   will feast on love divine.

4. By grace alone united,
   we join the heav'nly throng;
   with countless saints and martyrs,
   we sing the kingdom's song.
   'Oh holy, holy, holy!'
   the universe resounds
   with praise and adoration
   and endless grace abounds.

## 112 O Lord, how long

Michael Forster (b.1946)

Traditional melody
arr. Henri Friedrich Hémy (1818-1888)

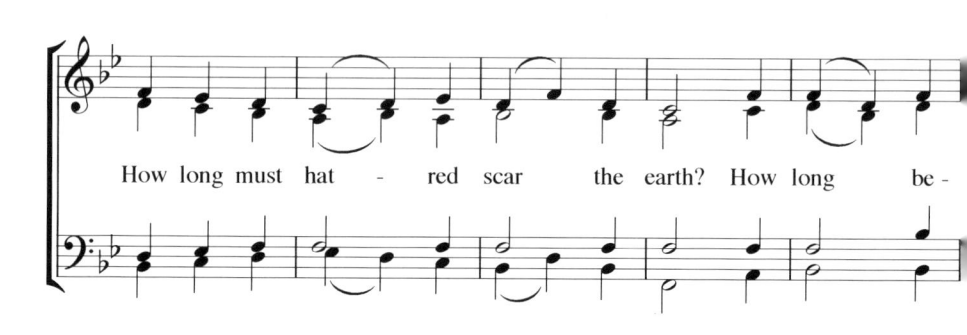

STELLA 88 88 88

1. O Lord, how long must fear pre-vail?
How long must hat-red scar the earth? How long be-fore your peo-ple learn the joy of love and hu-man worth? Spi-rit of God, Spi-rit of

Text © Copyright 2014 Kevin Mayhew Ltd.
*It is illegal to photocopy music.*

peace, from sin-ful pride our souls re-lease.

2. Give us the grace to start right here,
   with those with whom we disagree,
   help us to listen, learn and love,
   and prize our shared humanity.
   Spirit of God, Spirit of peace,
   from sinful pride our souls release.

3. Help us to take the risk of love
   and trust each other to be free;
   not to control or seek to change
   but revel in diversity.
   Spirit of God, Spirit of peace,
   from sinful pride our souls release.

4. Then let us, with reopened eyes,
   look out beyond our native lands
   to see the glory of your love
   in countless faces, hearts and hands.
   Spirit of God, Spirit of peace,
   from sinful pride our souls release.

5. And let us reach beyond our grasp
   to touch those hands in hope and peace,
   so war is made unthinkable
   and all our fear-full conflicts cease.
   Spirit of God, Spirit of peace,
   from sinful pride our souls release.

# 113 O Lord, you've searched me

Andrew Grinnell

Andrew Grinnell

1. O Lord, you've searched me and you know my heart, the words that I say, my inner-most thought. Your hand upon me is calming my fears, leading me on, wiping my tears.

2. All of my being was hand-made by you, creating my life to bring praise to you. You are revealing your will for my life, your plans are my hope, your love is my prize.

*Refrain*
There is no-

© Copyright 2000 Kevin Mayhew Ltd.
*It is illegal to photocopy music.*

# Sheet Music

| Em | D/F# | G | D/F# | Em | D/F# |

— where I can run to, to flee from your pre-sence, or

| G | D/F# | Em | D/F# | G | Bm7 |

hide from your truth. So I wait here for your Spi-rit to

| C | Asus4 | A | D | Gmaj7 |

guide me home to you. I re-joice at the cross and bow

| D | Gmaj7 | D | Gmaj7 |

down at your throne for your sac-ri-ficed Son has made

Bm7 A D Gmaj7
my sin his own. This is free-dom I've found, con-dem-
D Gmaj7 D Gmaj7
na-tion has gone, I'm your child, ho-ly King, I will
Bm A D.C. D
trust you a-lone.
Bm A D

*Songs for a*
SERVANT
CHURCH

# 114 O Love that searches all my soul

Susie Hare, based on Psalm 51:10-12

Susie Hare (b.1947)

POWNTLEY 86 86 86 866

**Unhurried**

1. O Love that search-es all my soul, cre-ate in me a-new, a pu-ri-fied and con-trite heart that search-es af-ter you. Je-sus, there is no sweet-er grace, nor such for-give-ness

© Copyright 2001 Kevin Mayhew Ltd.
*It is illegal to photocopy music.*

known as in the hum-ble hearts of those where-in your love is sown, where-in your love is sown.

2. O Love that washes all my sins,
   create in me anew,
   salvation's joy and peace restored
   as I abide in you.
   Jesus, there is no sweeter joy
   than that which grace revives,
   nor greater peace within my heart
   than heaven's love provides,
   than heaven's love provides.

3. O Love that lifts my voice to sing,
   create in me anew,
   a song that always fills my heart
   with thankfulness to you.
   Jesus, there is no sweeter song
   than that which breathes your name,
   and through eternity my praise
   will always be the same,
   will always be the same.

# 115 O West Bank town of Bethlehem

Martin E. Leckebusch (b.1962)
after Phillips Brooks (1835-1893)

Traditional English melody collected, adapted and arr. Ralph Vaughan Williams (1872-1958)

FOREST GREEN DCM

1. O West Bank town of Beth-le-hem, how still your vic-tims lie; the griev-ing weep, de-prived of sleep; mi-li-tia-men roam by; for through your dark streets rag - es the ne-ver-end-ing fight: such hopes and fears, such bit-ter tears are met in you to-night.

Text © Copyright 2010 Kevin Mayhew Ltd.
Music © from 'The English Hymnal'. Reproduced by permission of Oxford University Press. All rights reserved.
*It is illegal to photocopy music.*

2. O morning news, O papers,
   report the dreadful dearth
   of saints who sing to praise the King,
   of peace across the earth;
   where Christ was born of Mary
   'midst wond'ring angels' love,
   in anguish deep, sad mortals keep
   few thoughts of things above.

3. How violently, how violently
   the hope of peace is riv'n;
   can God impart to these torn hearts
   the blessings of his heav'n?
   Who now recalls his coming
   to this dark world of sin?
   Where harsh words still promote ill-will,
   can Christ now enter in?

4. O Child once born in Bethlehem,
   draw near again, we pray;
   you died to win this world from sin —
   yet sin persists today.
   May we, like Christmas angels,
   announce Immanuel,
   till all are giv'n a glimpse of heav'n
   and not a taste of hell.

## 116 One of us, flesh and blood

Garth Hewitt

Garth Hewitt

One of us, flesh and blood; reaching out, a touch of love: breaking walls that divide: God with us, bringing alive. God with live.

1. In a manger, in a cave, a humble
2. Had no place to lay his head, never
3. A child is born, a humble birth; a chance of

© Copyright 2012 Kevin Mayhew Ltd.
*It is illegal to photocopy music.*

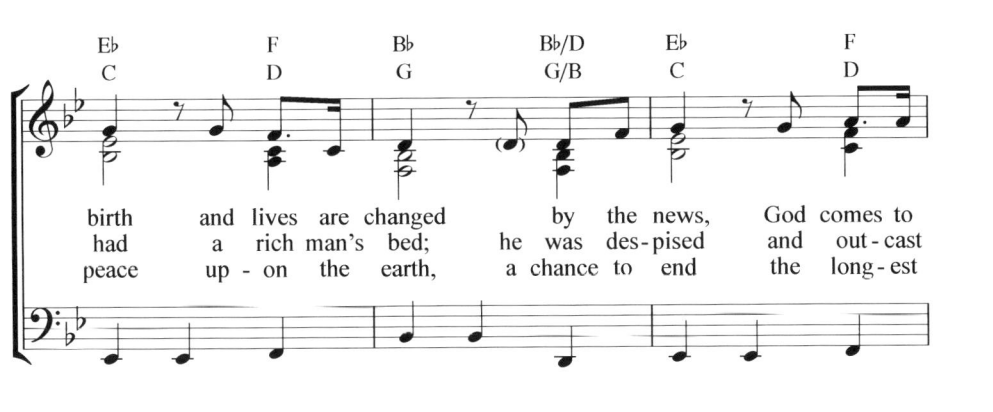

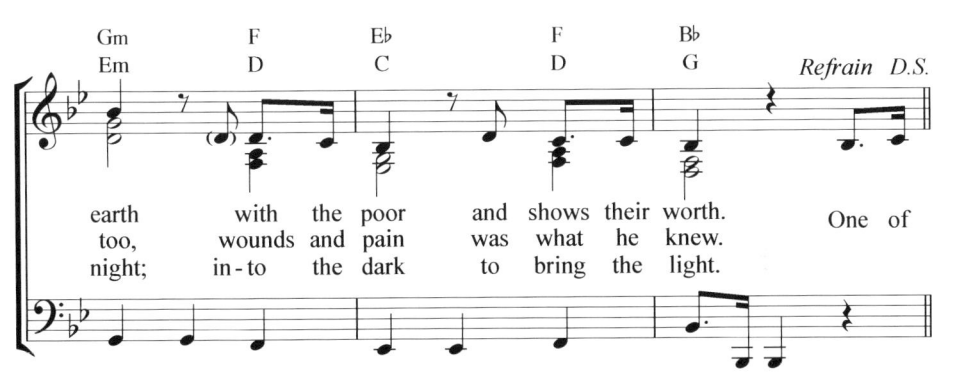

birth and lives are changed by the news, God comes to
had a rich man's bed; he was des-pised and out-cast
peace up-on the earth, a chance to end the long-est

earth with the poor and shows their worth. One of
too, wounds and pain was what he knew.
night; in-to the dark to bring the light.

*Refrain D.S.*

*Songs for a*
SERVANT
CHURCH

## 117 Open our eyes to see

Martin E. Leckebusch (b.1962)  Malcolm Archer (b.1953)

OPEN OUR EYES 66 66 44 44

1. Open our eyes to see
the anguish of the poor —
indignities untold
where life is insecure;
then may our ears discern your call
to demonstrate your care for all.

2. Open our minds to grasp
life's grim reality —
how greed and pow'r prolong
the curse of poverty;
and fill our mouths with words to speak,
defending those whose voice is weak.

3. Open our hands to give,
to serve through all our deeds,
and let our strength be spent
to meet our neighbours' needs;
let love, not duty, be our guide:
Lord, let our hearts be open wide!

© Copyright 1999 Kevin Mayhew Ltd.
*It is illegal to photocopy music.*

# 118 Open the door

Barbara Glasson

Rod Boucher
arr. Marian Hellen

Let the wel-come be lov-ing, not just for the poor. Cross the thresh-old of friend ship, o-pen the door.

2. Open the door, come critics, step in,
   those wounded by Christians, the profligate sons.

3. Open the door, let skeptics come in,
   the reasoned agnostic, the militant fringe.

4. Open the door, let fresh air blow through,
   fling back the shutters, discern something new.

5. Open the door, it swings on its hinge,
   from the voice of the doubtful, the truth can break in.

# Songs for a Servant Church

# 119 Our Father (Caribbean)

Christopher Massey
based on a traditional Caribbean text

Traditional Caribbean melody
arr. Keith Stent

1. Our Father, Father in heaven, *how we adore your name!* Your kingdom come, your will be done, *how we adore your name, how we adore your name!*

2. On earth as it is in heaven,
   *how we adore your name.*
   Give us this day our daily bread,
   *how we adore your name,*
   *how we adore your name!*

3. Forgive us for our wrong-doing,
   as we forgive when we are wronged.

4. Help us to resist temptation,
   deliver us from evil ways.

5. Yours, Father, yours is the kingdom,
   the glory and the pow'r, O Lord.

6. For ever, ever and ever,
   for evermore and evermore.

7. Amen, let it be forever,
   amen, amen for evermore.

Text © Copyright 2014 and this music arrangement
© Copyright 1999 Kevin Mayhew Ltd.
*It is illegal to photocopy music.*

# 120 Our Father in heaven

Susie Hare, based on the Lord's Prayer

Susie Hare (b.1947)

**Calypso**

Our Father in heaven, hallowed be your name, your kingdom come, your will be done on earth as in heaven. Give us today our daily bread. Forgive us our sins as we forgive

© Copyright 2001 Kevin Mayhew Ltd.
*It is illegal to photocopy music.*

C♭7 B♭7 E♭
B♭7 A7 D
those who sin a - gainst us. Lead us not in-to temp - ta -
Fm/E♭ B♭/E♭ E♭
Em/D A/D D
- tion, but de - liv - er us from e - vil. For the
Fm/E♭ B♭/E♭ E♭
Em/D A/D D
king - dom, the pow'r and the glo - ry are yours,
Fm Gm
Em F♯m
now and for e - ver, now and for e - ver,
A♭ A♭/B♭ B♭7 E♭
G G/A A7 D
now and for e - ver. A - men.

# 121 Out of the darkness of the night
*Wonderful, glorious day.*

Susie Hare                                                          Susie Hare (b.1947)

84 84 88 87 and Refrain

1. Out of the dark-ness of the night    Je-sus    called me.
2. Out of a life    of guilt and sin    Je-sus    called me.
3. No great-er sac-ri-fice was made:    Je-sus    made it.

In-to the ra-diance of his light    Je-sus    brought me,
In-to a life    that hon-ours him    Je-sus    brought me,
No great-er debt    was e-ver paid:    Je-sus    paid it.

© Copyright 2015 Kevin Mayhew Ltd.
*It is illegal to photocopy music.*

giv - ing my life a brand new start, chang-ing my cold and stub-born heart.
choos-ing this sin - ner for his own, mak-ing this hum - ble heart his home,
No great-er love, no great - er grace; bear-ing the cross, he took my place.

Now I am his a - dop - ted child,
Now I am his, I'm jus - ti - fied —
Now I'm for - giv - en, now I'm free,

res - cued, ran - somed, re - con - ciled!
pur - chased, par - doned, pu - ri - fied!
all be - cause he died for me.

*Refrain (twice to end)*
Won - der - ful, glo - ri - ous day! Je - sus saved me,

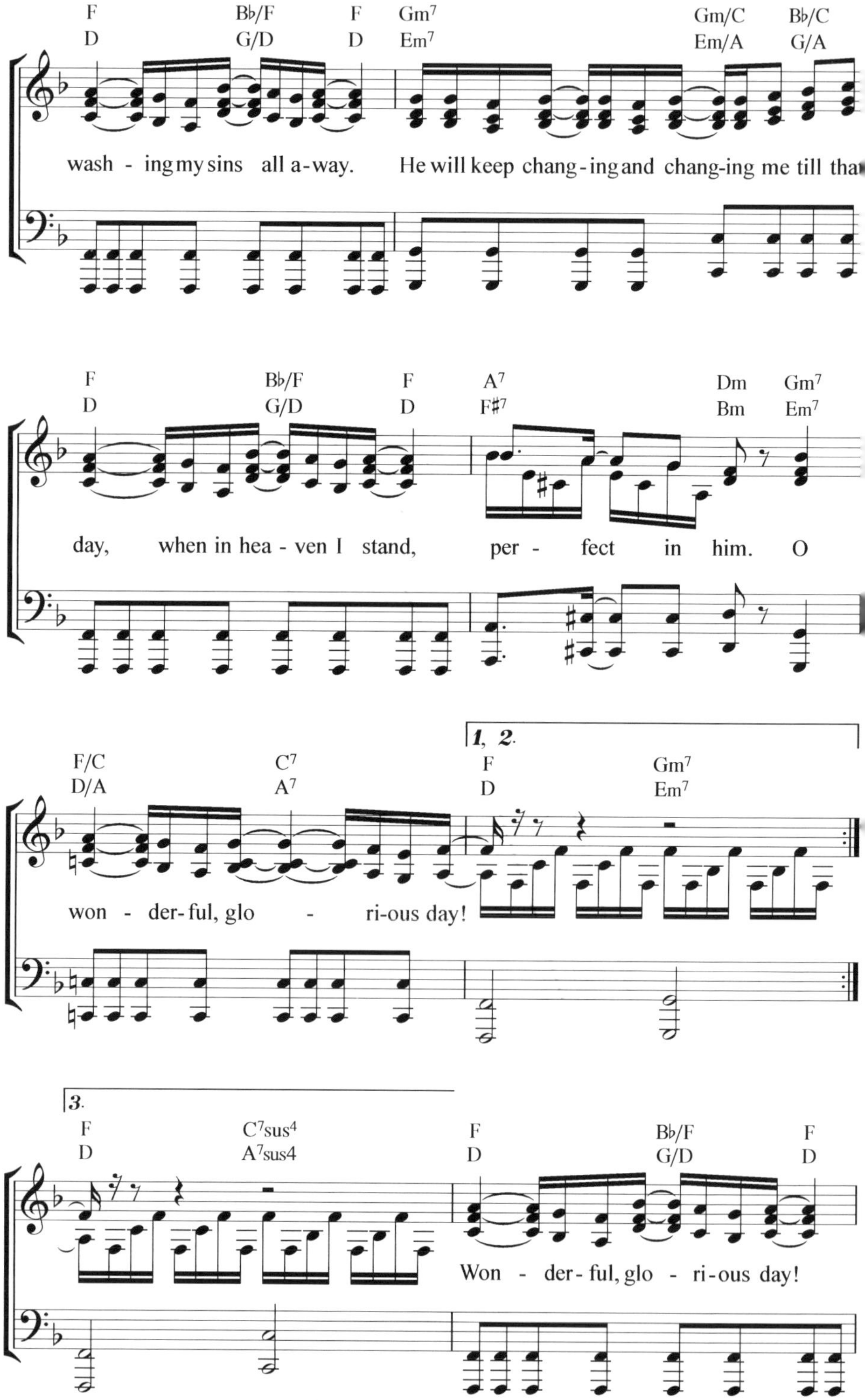

F Bb/F F Gm7 Gm/C Bb/C
D G/D D Em7 Em/A G/A
wash - ing my sins all a-way. He will keep chang-ing and chang-ing me till that
F Bb/F F A7 Dm Gm7
D G/D D F#7 Bm Em7
day, when in hea - ven I stand, per - fect in him. O
F/C C7
D/A A7
1, 2.
F Gm7
D Em7
won - der-ful, glo - ri-ous day!
3.
F C7sus4 F Bb/F F
D A7sus4 D G/D D
Won - der-ful, glo - ri-ous day!

B♭/F F F/C C F B♭/F F
G/D D D/A A D G/D D
Je - sus saved me, wash - ing my sins all a - way.
Gm Gm/C B♭/C
Em Em/A G/A
He will keep chang - ing and chang - ing me till that
F B♭/F F
D G/D D
day, when in hea - ven I stand,
A7 Dm Gm7 F/C C7
F♯7 Bm Em7 D/A A7
per - fect in him. O won - der - ful, glo - ri - ous day!
Dm Fmaj7/C B♭ Gm7 F/C C7 F
Bm Dmaj7/A G Em7 D/A A7 D
Slower
O won - der - ful, glo - ri - ous day!

# 122 People, look east

Martin E. Leckebusch (b.1962)

Traditional French melody
arr. Donald Thomson

BESANÇON CAROL 87 98 87

1. People, look east to see at last hopes fulfilled from ages past: now in the promise of the morning, see, a brighter day is dawning, rich with the visions long foretold, prophets' dreams from days of old.

Text © Copyright 2000, and this music arrangement
© Copyright 2014 Kevin Mayhew Ltd.
*It is illegal to photocopy music.*

2. God reaffirms the gracious call:
   words of welcome meant for all;
   comfort enough for all our sorrows;
   justice shaping new tomorrows.
   Mercy bears fruit in lives restored,
   freed to praise and serve the Lord.

3. Now, with the coming of the light,
   darkest fears are put to flight;
   see how the clouds of gloom are clearing,
   blown aside by hope's appearing.
   Jesus, the Light of all our days,
   comes and sets our hearts ablaze.

4. Born of our race, a child so small —
   hail the promised Lord of all!
   Nailed to a cross for our salvation,
   he shall rule God's new creation.
   Lift up your eyes, and look again:
   see, he comes in pow'r to reign!

## 123 Praise to Christ, the Lord incarnate

Martin E. Leckebusch (b.1962)          Graham Kendrick (b.1950)

**Steadily**
*Unison*

1. Praise to Christ, the Lord in-car-nate, gift of God by hu-man birth: he it is who came a-mong us, shared our life and showed our worth; ours the tur-moil he en-coun-tered, ours the griefs he made his own; now with-in our hearts his Spi-rit makes his way of free-dom known.

Text © Copyright 2000 Kevin Mayhew Ltd.
Music © Copyright 2002 Make Way Music. www.grahamkendrick.co.uk. Used by permission.
*It is illegal to photocopy music.*

2. Praise to Christ, the Man of Sorrows,
tasting death for our release:
his the cup of bitter anguish,
ours the pardon, ours the peace;
his the blood that seals forgiveness,
ours the weight of guilt he bore —
so by death and resurrection
Christ has opened heaven's door.

3. Praise to Christ, the Priest eternal:
still for us he intercedes;
still he sees our pains and problems —
how he understands our needs!
Yesterday, today, forever,
always he remains the same:
pledged to bring us to the Father,
strong in grace, and free from blame.

# 124 Room prepared; disciples meet

*Jesus came to save us*

Peter Dainty (b.1936)  
Geoffrey Nobes (b.1954)

JESUS CAME TO SAVE US 77 76

1. Room prepared; disciples meet; bowl and towel, washing feet; God's plan ready to complete — Jesus came to save us.

2. Broken

Text © Copyright 2009 and Music  
© Copyright 2014 Kevin Mayhew Ltd.  
*It is illegal to photocopy music.*

2. Broken bread and poured out wine;
   holy body, blood divine;
   was there ever food so fine? —
   Jesus came to save us.

3. Midnight garden, olive wood,
   pray'rs of anguish, sweat like blood;
   he accepts the will of God —
   Jesus came to save us.

4. Priestly pride and Roman pow'r;
   soldiers' lash; spectators' jeer;
   now has come his finest hour —
   Jesus came to save us.

5. Wounded flesh and flowing blood;
   sharp the nails and rough the wood;
   he reveals the love of God —
   Jesus came to save us.

6. Linen cloth and borrowed tomb;
   spices mask the smell of doom;
   earth can give him no more room —
   Jesus came to save us.

7. Empty grave, angelic light;
   friends bewildered by the sight;
   he has ended death's dark night —
   Jesus came to save us.

# 125 Sad, confused and shaken

Nick Fawcett (b.1957)        Betty Roe (b.1930)

KELFIELD 65 65 D

1. Sad, con-fused and sha - ken, Ma - ry stood a - lone,
all her dreams in ru - ins, bu - ried in a tomb.
Then a stran - ger met her, call - ing her by name,
tears gave way to laugh - ter, life be - gan a - gain.

© Copyright 2000 Kevin Mayhew Ltd.
*It is illegal to photocopy music.*

2. Sad, confused and shaken,
   two friends wandered home,
   all their dreams in ruins,
   buried in a tomb.
   Then a stranger met them,
   offered bread and wine,
   shattered faith rekindled,
   light began to shine.

3. Sad, confused and shaken,
   friends locked in a room,
   all their dreams in ruins,
   buried in a tomb.
   Then their Master met them,
   standing by their side,
   risen and victorious,
   Jesus who had died!

4. Sad, confused and shaken,
   we may sometimes be,
   all our dreams in ruins,
   hopelessly at sea.
   But don't be defeated,
   let hope spring anew,
   for the risen Jesus
   waits to meet with you.

# 126 Saviour, precious Saviour

Geoffrey Nobes  
Geoffrey Nobes (b.1954)

1. Saviour, precious Saviour, you are here with us now,
sharing our joy and our love;
ready to receive us, to forgive and to heal,
bringing your truth from above.

2. Saviour, precious Saviour, you have called us by name,
caring and making us whole;
giving without measure, you restore and renew,
filling the heart and the soul.

© Copyright 2014 Kevin Mayhew Ltd.
*It is illegal to photocopy music.*

*Refrain*

Your love for me makes me all I want to be,
ev-'ry mo-ment with you by my side;
your grace so free gives me strength and li-ber-ty,
pre-cious Sa-viour, my friend and guide.

## 127 Set the sail on your boat

Barbara Glasson

Rod Boucher
arr. Marian Heller

**Gently and loosely**

1. Set the sail on your boat to the soft morning air, let the dawn's gentle wisp move you onward. 2. Let the quiet early

*Refrain*
You may feel all adrift on the wide ocean's

© Copyright 2015 Kevin Mayhew Ltd.
*It is illegal to photocopy music.*

2. Let the quiet early gust
   take the breath from your lungs,
   feel the longing for life
   drive you windward.

3. But you're free as the gulls
   on the eddies above.
   You are buoyed by the tide,
   pushing forward.

4. You will know the deep peace
   of a love whispered breeze,
   as the spirit will blow
   on and outward.

5. Yet each breath that you draw
   brings a voice to explore.
   It's the voice that is truth
   calling inward.

6. Set the sail on your boat
   to the soft morning air,
   let the dawn's gentle wisp
   move you onward.

# 128 Sing 'Hey!' for the God who is eternally new
*God's surprise*

Michael Forster (b.1946)

Joseph Brackett (1797-1882)
arr. Donald Thomson

SIMPLE GIFTS 12 12 12 10 and Refrain

1. Sing 'Hey!' for the God who is eternally new, who leads in the search to discover what is true, as old as the mountains, yet as fresh as the dawn, and always and ev'rywhere newly born.

Text © Copyright 2014 Kevin Mayhew Ltd.
This music arrangement © Copyright 2016 Kevin Mayhew Ltd.
*It is illegal to photocopy music.*

2. The God who surrenders to creation's embrace,
   who baffles the wise with the foolishness of grace,
   whose wealth can be wafted on the wings of a dove,
   who trusts in no pow'r but the pow'r of love.

3. The God who conceives us and who brings us to birth,
   delights in our play and assures us of our worth,
   who watches and wonders through the youngest of eyes,
   and chuckles with glee at each new surprise.

4. The God who accompanies the dance that is life,
   through gardens and deserts, through harmony and strife,
   who journeys before us through the darkness of death,
   to dance in the dawn of eternal breath.

5. Sing 'Hey!' for the people who by grace we might be,
   from stigma delivered, from prejudice set free,
   to see and to celebrate, in ev'ryone's face,
   eternally new and suprising grace.

# 129 Sing, my tongue, the glorious struggle

Christopher Massey

Plainsong mode iii
arr. Andrew Moore

TUNE 1: PANGE LINGUA 87 87 87

1. Sing, my tongue, the glorious struggle,
of the final vict'ry sing;
o-ver that great cross, his trophy,
let the Saviour's praises ring:
tell how he, the world's Redeemer,
conquered death through suffering.

A - men.

2. At the time by God appointed,
for the saving of our race,
he forsook the realms of glory
for the world of time and space,
in the Virgin's womb uniting
mortal flesh and holy grace.

3. With the thirty years accomplished,
passionate in deed and word,
willingly the Word embraces
crucifixion, spear and sword.
On the cross the lamb is lifted,
and atoning life-blood poured.

4. Taste the bitter gall of hatred,
wine fermented from our fear;
see the holy body, opened
by the nails, the thorns and spear!
Watch in awe, as blood and water
wash the whole creation clear.

This version of text © Copyright 2014, and this music arrangement
© Copyright 1996 Kevin Mayhew Ltd.
*It is illegal to photocopy music.*

**PART TWO**

5. Faithful Cross, above all other,
   one and only noble tree,
   standing strong, all things enduring,
   bearing fruit abundantly;
   you alone this weight can carry
   with divine serenity.

6. Bend and stretch your limbs and branches
   reaching over land and sea,
   so that all the world may witness
   love's expense and agony;
   heaven's Highest, earth's Redeemer,
   born aloft to set us free.

7. You alone could bear the burden
   of creation's dying Lord;
   be the ark that saved creation
   while the chaos-waters roared;
   with the blood of life anointed,
   from the Lamb of God outpoured.

8. Praise and honour to the Father,
   praise and honour to the Son,
   with the all-embracing Spirit,
   fully Three and wholly One;
   One in love's eternal glory,
   One before all things begun.

TUNE 2: ST THOMAS (WEBBE) 87 87 87         Samuel Webbe (1740-1816)

1. Sing, my tongue, the glorious struggle, of the final vict'ry sing;
o - ver that great cross, his tro - phy, let the Saviour's prai - ses ring:
tell how he, the world's Re - deem - er, con - quered death through suf - fer - ing.

# Songs *for a* SERVANT CHURCH

# 130 Sing the gospel of salvation

Michael Forster (b.1946)          Charles Crozat Converse (1832-1918)

WHAT A FRIEND (CONVERSE) 87 87 D

1. Sing the gospel of salvation, tell it out to all the earth;
to the ones so long excluded, speak of hope and human worth.
All the darkness of injustice cannot dim salvation's light,
for the outcast and exploited count as worthy in God's sight.

2. Christ, the great eternal Shepherd,
calls creation to rejoice,
and the victims of oppression
thrill to hear salvation's voice.
All who hear and recognise him,
take their place within the fold,
there, in perfect truth and freedom,
life's eternal joys to hold.

3. See, the host that none can number
gathers in from ev'ry side,
once the victims of injustice,
now redeemed and glorified.
Fear and weeping here are ended,
hunger and oppression cease.
Now the Lamb becomes the Shepherd!
Now begins the reign of peace!

Text © Copyright 1993 Kevin Mayhew Ltd.
*It is illegal to photocopy music.*

# 131 Sound out his praises

Nick Fawcett (b.1957)

George Frideric Handel (1685-1759)
arr. Colin Hand

HANDEL 10 10 66 10 8

1. Sound out his prai- ses, for God has blessed us with love so pre- cious; his love a- maz- es! His hands have shaped the earth, brought light and life to birth, our world, so rich and full, he made it all. Lift up your voice and praise the Lord. Lord.

*To next verse*

*Last time*

Text and this music arrangement
© Copyright 2000 Kevin Mayhew Ltd.
*It is illegal to photocopy music.*

2. Sound out his praises, in exultation
   and jubilation; his love amazes!
   The earth, the sea, the sky,
   the firmament on high;
   the universe so vast; he made it all.
   Lift up your voice and praise the Lord.

3. Sound out his praises, in glad rejoicing,
   your worship voicing; his love amazes!
   The sights, the scents, the touch,
   the tastes, the sounds — so much —
   this earth, so wonderful — he made it all.
   Lift up your voice and praise the Lord.

4. Sound out his praises, with heartfelt gladness;
   away with sadness; his love amazes!
   The love which thrills our hearts,
   the joys each day imparts,
   the precious gift of life; he made it all.
   Lift up your voice and praise the Lord.

# 132 Such a host as none can number

Michael Forster (b.1946)  
Richard Runciman Terry (1865-1938)  
adapted by Alan Ridou

RUNCIMAN 87 87 D and Refrain

1. Such a host as none can number, ev-'ry tribe and ev-'ry race, robed be-fore the Lamb in glo-ry, ga-ther at the throne of grace. 'To our God a-scribe sal-va-tion, glo-ry to the Lamb be-longs.' All the saints, in one com-mu-nion, join the glad tri-um-phal song:

© Copyright 1992 Kevin Mayhew Ltd.  
*It is illegal to photocopy music.*

*Refrain*

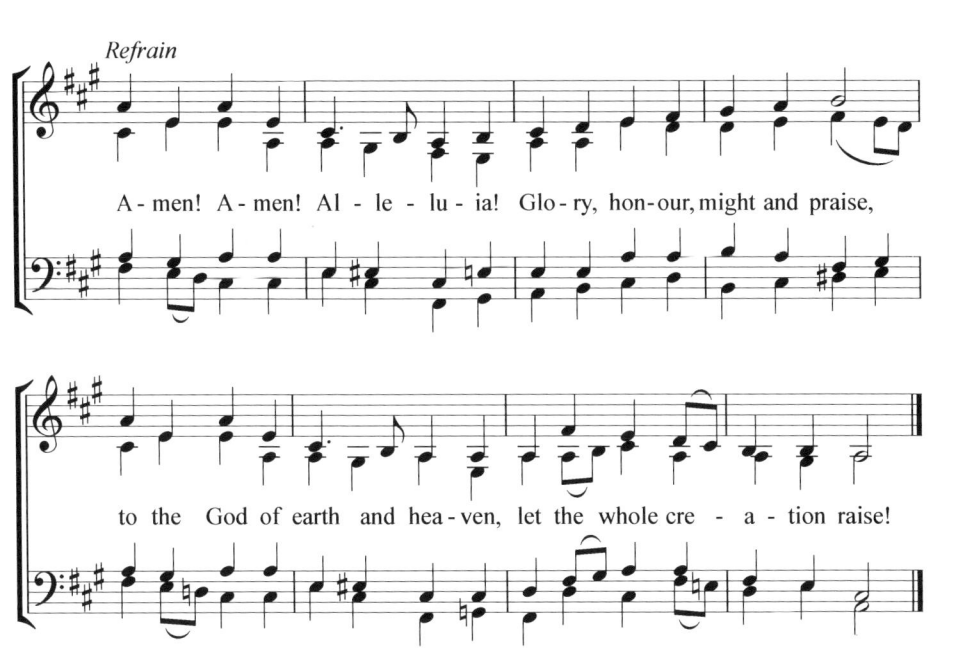

A-men! A-men! Al-le-lu-ia! Glo-ry, hon-our, might and praise, to the God of earth and hea-ven, let the whole cre-a-tion raise!

2. Those who suffered great injustice,
   now redeemed and glorified,
   day and night their praises offer
   to the Lamb once crucified.
   No more shall they thirst and hunger,
   no more fear the scorching heat,
   for the Lamb will be their shepherd,
   ev'ry need and longing meet.

3. See this vision of the future
   put to shame the world we know!
   Hear the heav'nly choirs protesting
   with the victims here below.
   Heal the sick and feed the hungry,
   strive to set the captive free.
   In the presence of the future,
   this our joyful song shall be:

# 133 Teach me, dear Lord

Martin E. Leckebusch (b.1962)

Traditional Irish melody
transcr. Jane Ross (1810-1879)
arr. Noel Rawsthorne

DANNY BOY 11 10 11 10 11 10 11 12

1. Teach me, dear Lord, to savour ev-'ry moment— each precious hour, a gift which is unique— for your unhurried guiding hand I cherish and the contentment of your ways I seek. When date and

*Text © Copyright 2000 and this music arrangement*
*© Copyright 1996 Kevin Mayhew Ltd.*
*It is illegal to photocopy music.*

time de-mand my full at-ten-tion from fran-tic rush-ing let my heart be free, that I may flow with-in your Spi rit's rhy-thm and live each min-ute just as it was meant to be.

2. But may I also glimpse the broader canvas —
to all my life, a purpose and a plan —
and let me hear again that voice which called me
before this world or time itself began.
So may your kingdom daily be my watchword
and may the pulse in all my life be praise,
across unfolding years and changing seasons,
until with you I walk through everlasting days.

# 134 Teach us how to walk — *Dance on injustice*

Garth Hewitt

1. Teach us how to walk in your footsteps, Jesus, teach us how to walk in your way. Teach us how to show your love to our neighbour, teach us how to do it today. And we will dance, dance, dance, dance on injustice, we will

2. Teach us how to see through your eyes, Jesus,
   teach us how to love the poor.
   Give us your heart as you see the hungry,
   and teach us how to love them more.

3. Teach us how to see through your eyes, Jesus,
   to stand with the refugee.
   And those whose land has been taken from them,
   the forgotten ones we fail to see.

4. Teach us how to break the walls of injustice,
   teach us how to make a stand.
   Teach us how to build a community of peace,
   where love has the upper hand.

5. We dance today to thank you, Jesus,
   you give us hope to sing.
   You dance beside us in the battle for justice,
   and justice is going to win.

## 135 Tell, my tongue, the awesome mystery

Christopher Massey

Plainsong mode iii
arr. Andrew Moore

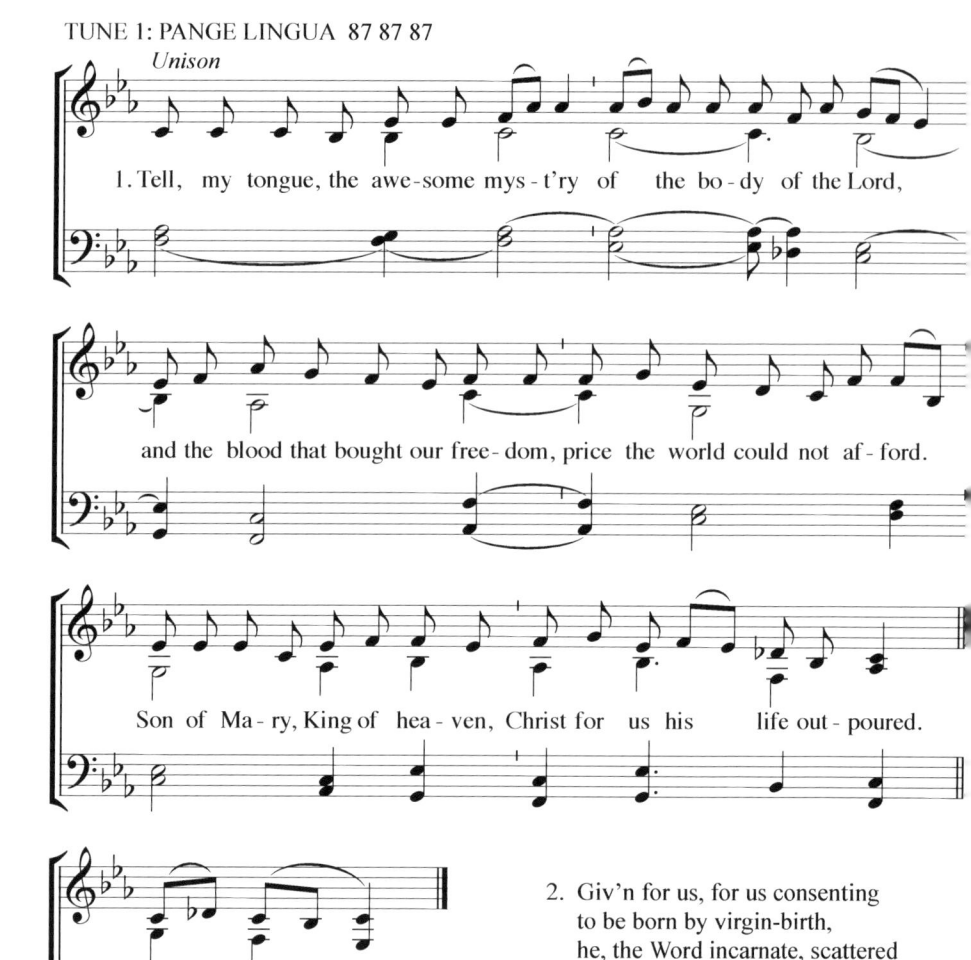

TUNE 1: PANGE LINGUA 87 87 87

1. Tell, my tongue, the awesome myst'ry of the body of the Lord,
and the blood that bought our freedom, price the world could not afford.
Son of Mary, King of heaven, Christ for us his life outpoured.

A - men.

2. Giv'n for us, for us consenting
to be born by virgin-birth,
he, the Word incarnate, scattered
gospel seed upon the earth,
showing, in his life among us,
love divine and human worth.

3. At his table then reclining,
with the Twelve, the chosen few,
he, the ancient feast fulfilling,
shared the Passover anew,
then, revealing love's true glory,
led the way death's curtain through.

4. Word-made-flesh true bread is making
into flesh by word and sign;
and the blood that saves creation
is revealed in sacred wine.
Faith alone, when senses falter,
sees the mystery divine.

This version of text © Copyright 2014, and this music arrangement
© Copyright 1996 Kevin Mayhew Ltd.
*It is illegal to photocopy music.*

5. Let us come with awe and wonder
   to this sacrament of grace,
   as the code of law and judgement
   give to love the pride of place;
   at the limits of our senses,
   faith transcends both time and space.

6. Praise and honour now be given
   to the Father and the Son,
   with the all-embracing Spirit,
   fully Three and wholly One.
   Glory, honour, praise and blessing
   while unending ages run.

TUNE 2: TANTUM ERGO (GRAFTON) 87 87 87      French melody (1881)

1. Tell, my tongue, the awesome myst'ry of the body of the Lord, and the blood that bought our freedom, price the world could not afford. Son of Mary, King of heaven, Christ for us his life outpoured.

# 136 The day will come, that glorious day

Martin E. Leckebusch (b.1962)      Kevin Mayhew (b.1942)

MULTICOLOURED TAPESTRY 88 88 D

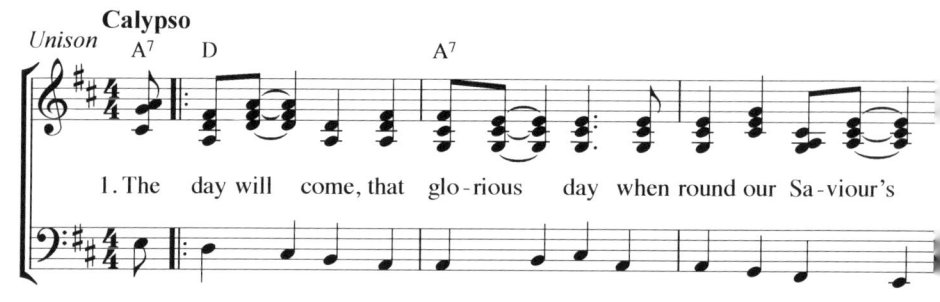

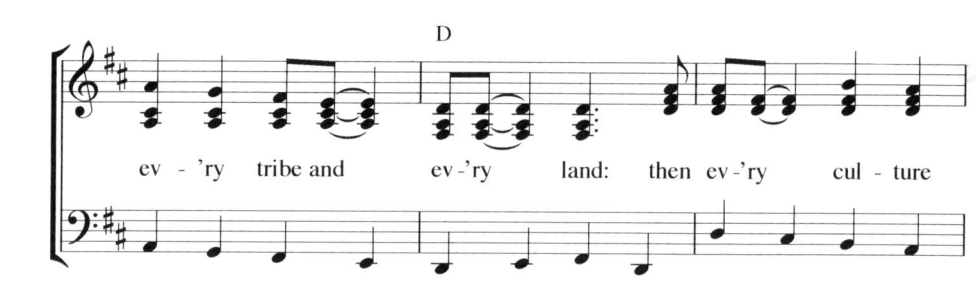

*Calypso*

1. The day will come, that glorious day when round our Saviour's throne we stand, a multitude too vast to count, from ev-'ry tribe and ev-'ry land: then ev-'ry culture will provide its own distinctive offering, some

© Copyright 2013 Kevin Mayhew Ltd.
*It is illegal to photocopy music.*

fa-cet   of   the   grace of   God,   some in - sight   no one   else can   bring.   2. This   ev-'ry   face.
3. So

2. This carnival of joy and praise,
   this multicoloured tapestry,
   is now foreshadowed in the Church
   with all its rich diversity:
   no skin-deep diff'rence can deny
   the unity where all belong —
   our voices, when they blend as one,
   enhance the beauty of our song.

3. So fan the vision into flame!
   Affirm the heights of human worth!
   Deny the scourge of prejudice
   its final refuge on the earth!
   Let no one be refused the chance
   to probe in depth the call of grace:
   God's kingdom seen in daily life,
   God's glory lighting ev'ry face.

# 137 The gracious invitation

Martin E. Leckebusch (b.1962)        Kevin Mayhew (b.1942)

**MONKS ELEIGH DCM**

1. The gracious invitation stands for any who will come; the Father runs with open arms to children heading home — and all who trudge with weary feet along life's dusty road receive at last a welcome chance to lose their heavy

© Copyright 2013 Kevin Mayhew Ltd.
*It is illegal to photocopy music.*

2. No longer need we clothe our lives
   in garments soiled and torn
   when Christ gives robes of righteousness
   for what was old and worn:
   to those bereft of dignity
   and yearning to be whole,
   forgiveness brings the healing pow'r
   which liberates the soul.

3. When all that busy lives produce
   is dry futility,
   we find in Christ the living source
   of full reality;
   and if, within our hearts, the truth
   is what we long to hear,
   the whisper of the Spirit comes
   as music to the ear.

4. Whoever looks for nourishment
   will find the table spread:
   the finest riches heaven holds,
   foretold in wine and bread.
   The banquet is for ev'ryone,
   the greatest and the least:
   for all are called as honoured guests
   to come and join the feast!

## 138 The heavens proclaim God's glory

Martin E. Leckebusch (b.1962)  
George James Webb (1803-1887)

MORNING LIGHT 76 76 D

1. The heav'ns proclaim God's glory, the skies sing out in praise, extolling their creator through endless nights and days. More eloquent than language, more radiant than the sun, this message of God's splendour is meant for ev'ry-one.

2. The law of God is perfect,
its precepts always right,
revealing timeless wisdom,
providing life and light —
no gold could be so precious,
no honey taste as sweet;
and those who yield obedience
will find their joy complete.

3. Forgive my secret failures,
the faults I do not know;
from wilful sins protect me,
and ways I should not go.
May all my meditations,
my ev'ry thought and word,
be fashioned for your pleasure,
my Saviour and my Lord.

Text © Copyright 2001 Kevin Mayhew Ltd.
*It is illegal to photocopy music.*

# 139 The Lord created family

Martin E. Leckebusch (b.1962)

Brother James Macbeth Bain (d.1925)
arr. Colin Mawby

BROTHER JAMES' AIR CM

1. The Lord cre-a-ted fa-mi-ly to make his kind-ness known: for when we care the way we ought our love re-flects his own — a love which al-ways reach-es out to those who feel a-lone.

2. Give thanks for all the families
which function as they should,
whose members make it their delight
to do each other good —
for homes which truly demonstrate
the Father's fatherhood.

3. But pray for those whose families
are torn apart by strife —
where pressure mounts, where love is scarce,
where arguments are rife —
that God will heal their brokenness
and so enrich their life.

4. The Lord has made a family
with members ev'rywhere,
and Jesus is the eldest Son,
the one whose name we bear —
whose words and life show holiness,
a likeness we can share.

5. We are your Church, your family,
the children of your grace:
inspire us, Lord, to show this world
the warmth of your embrace
till all who long for wholeness find
a welcome and a place.

Text © Copyright 1999, and this music arrangement
© Copyright 2004 Kevin Mayhew Ltd.
*It is illegal to photocopy music.*

# 140 The Lord reveals his glory

Martin E. Leckebusch (b.1962)

Traditional Irish melody
arr. Christopher Tambling

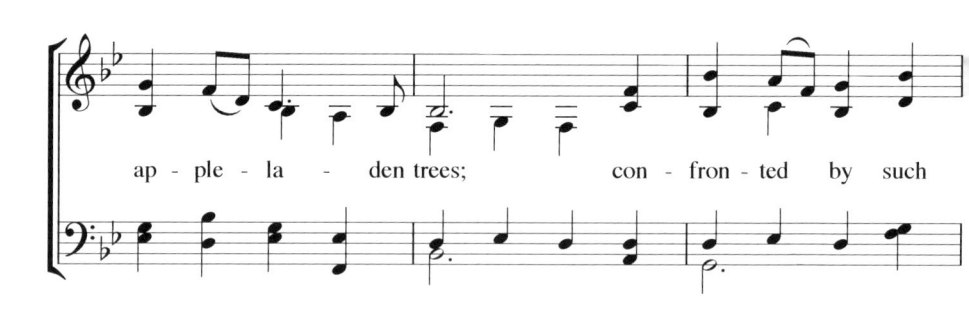

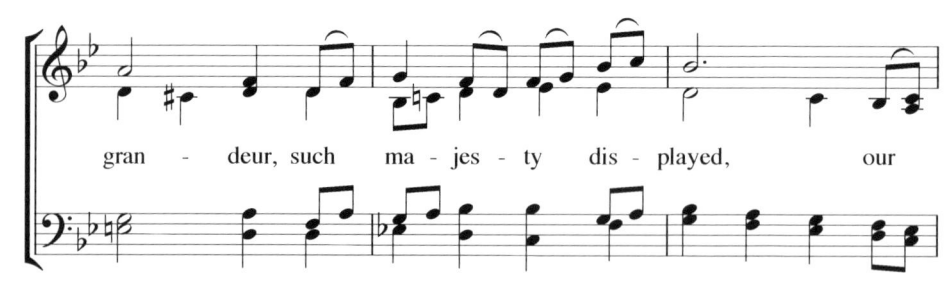

SALLEY GARDENS 76 76 D

1. The Lord reveals his glory in raging winter seas, in swans and supernovas; in apple-laden trees; confronted by such grandeur, such majesty displayed, our

Text © Copyright 2010, and this music arrangement
© Copyright 2007 Kevin Mayhew Ltd.
*It is illegal to photocopy music.*

hearts ex - plode with wor - ship for all our God has made.

2. The Lord reveals his glory
   in fire beyond all flame,
   in light beyond all brightness,
   in wonders none can name.
   His deep, eternal thunder
   evokes our rev'rent fear;
   he shouts in words and silence
   the truth we need to hear.

3. The Lord reveals his glory
   in lives attuned to grace,
   where hope dispels the shadow
   from any human face,
   where visions born of justice
   bear fruit in dignity
   and neighbours serve each other
   with glad humility.

4. The Lord reveals his glory
   within the attitude
   of lives which bear the hallmark
   of honest gratitude;
   so may our skills and labours
   be honed to build aright
   a world to show God's glory,
   a world for God's delight.

# 141 The man of the margins

Barbara Glasson

Rod Bouche
arr. Marian Heller

*Rolling*

*Refrain*

The man of the mar-gins says

'Hey! There's a mar-gin of doubt be-tween pro-ven and real and a mar-gin for er-ror in cer-tain-ty. There's a mar-gin of risk be-tween trust-ing and doubt and a mar-gin for grace in ad-ver-si-ty.'

*Last time to Coda*

1. Are you strange or de-ranged, has your brain been short changed, a

© Copyright 2015 Kevin Mayhew Ltd.
*It is illegal to photocopy music.*

2. Are you poor any more, is that wolf at the door,
   is this pile of bad debts all your fault?
   Have you mislaid your pills or just not paid the bills?
   What is it the money men say?

3. Are you guilty or clean, what's the view at the scene,
   are the fingerprints pointing at you?
   It's a difficult age, were you driven by rage?
   What is it the legal reps say?

4. Are you homeless or cheat, what's the word on the street?
   Are you user or dealer, what's true?
   Is there credit or doubt on your need to sleep out?
   What is it the officers say?

5. Are you righteous or flawed, can your past be ignored,
   are you saintly or tarnished right through?
   Are you on the right side of salvation's divide?
   What is it the church-goers say?

## 142 The only power that cleanses me

Susie Hare  
Susie Hare (b.1947)

1. The only pow'r that cleanses me is in the blood of Jesus, and as I look to Calvary, his sacrifice I see. And
2. The only love that sets me free is in the heart of Jesus; a heart so full of tenderness and faithfulness to me. And
3. I never cease to be amazed that he should love so dearly, a child of such unworthiness, a sinner such as me. And

anything that I might give would always be too

Gsus4 G C C7 F C/E
small to e - ver pay the debt I owe to
Dm7 C/E F C/E Dm7 Gsus4 G7
him who gave his life for me, to him who gave me
1, 2.
C Fadd2 Dm7 Gsus4 G
all.
3.
C C F G
2. The all. So Je - sus, take this
3. I

C G/B Am F C/E Gsus4 G
thank - ful heart, al - though my gift is small. And
C C7 F C/E Dm7 C/E
I will live to wor - ship you, be - cause you gave your
F C/E Dm7 Gsus4 G C
life for me, be - cause you gave me all.
Fadd2 Dm7 Gsus4 G C
rall.

# 143 The path is stony
## *Lord, close to you*

Sean Bowman (1943-2013)          Geoffrey Nobes (b.1954)

1. The path is stony, rough and mean,
   Lord, without you;
   the road is winding, end unseen,
   Lord, without you.
   Give me, Lord, your light, I pray,
   show the straight and narrow way,
   keep me, when I go astray,
   Lord, close to you.

2. The night is black and full of fears,
   Lord, without you;
   my sleep disturbed and full of tears,
   Lord, without you.
   Give me, Lord, your peace, I pray,
   soothe tormented thoughts away,
   all my doubts and fears allay,
   Lord, close to you.

3. When life is aimless, empty, bleak,
   Lord, without you;
   temptation filled, my spirit weak,
   Lord, without you.
   Give me, Lord, your strength, I pray,
   grant me grace that I may stay,
   ev'ry hour of ev'ry day,
   Lord, close to you.

© Copyright 2014 Kevin Mayhew Ltd.
*It is illegal to photocopy music.*

# 144 The promised time arrives

Martin E. Leckebusch (b.1962)      Geoffrey Beaumont (1903-1970)

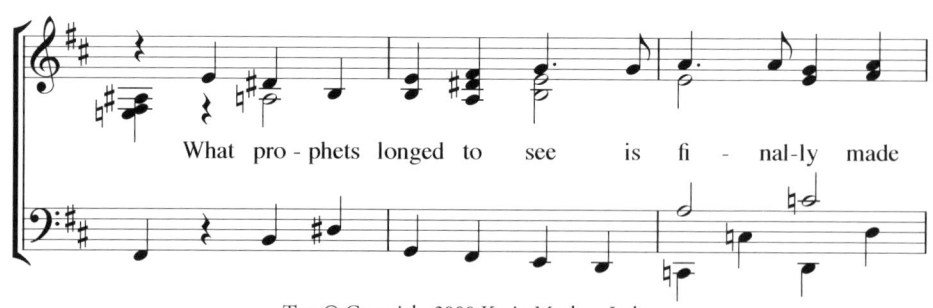

GRACIAS 67 67 66 66

1. The promised time arrives, the time of God's appointing — the time when One is born who bears the Lord's anointing. What prophets longed to see is finally made

Text © Copyright 2000 Kevin Mayhew Ltd.
Music © Copyright 1965 Paxton Music Ltd. Used by permission of Novello & Co. Ltd.
All rights reserved. International copyright secured.
*It is illegal to photocopy music.*

May also be sung to 'Nun Danket'

2. Unnumbered angels sing
in joyful acclamation,
for Christ the Lord is born,
the bringer of salvation;
there in a manger lies
the Lord of heav'n and earth,
who dignifies our life
by sharing human birth.

3. He comes as David's Heir
and Abraham's Descendant,
yet takes no worldly throne
with royal gold resplendent;
though rulers seek him out
to worship or to slay,
no pow'r devised on earth
can take his crown away.

4. The way to God he shows
to all who will receive him —
what light and life are ours
if we will but believe him!
The Son of God is here,
so full of truth and grace —
God's glory is disclosed
upon a human face.

# 145 The Spirit of God — *Good news to the poor*

Michael Forster (b.1946) — June Nixon

ST KILDA 55 55 65 65

1. The Spirit of God on us has been poured: the oil of his love; the fire of his word. While dwelling within us, he travels before and calls us to carry good news to the poor, and calls us to carry good news to the poor.

© Copyright 1992 Kevin Mayhew Ltd.
*It is illegal to photocopy music.*

2. The gospel we tell is wholeness and light:
   of captives released; of blind given sight.
   Oppressed will be freed by the pow'r of the word,
   proclaiming as present the day of the Lord,
   proclaiming as present the day of the Lord.

3. Oh fill us with hope, impatient to see
   the broken made whole, the captive set free,
   till justice and mercy to all points extend,
   the whole earth cry 'Glory!' and joy never end,
   the whole earth cry 'Glory!' and joy never end.

# 146 The Tango of our lives

Barbara Glasson

Rod Boucher
arr. Marian Hellen

**Vibrantly**

1. Find-ing the tem-po in-side the dis-cord. Not-ing the move-ment, with-in the long-ings. Shift-ing the bal-ance, puls-es and bod-ies. Tap-ping the Tan-go of our

© Copyright 2015 Kevin Mayhew Ltd.
*It is illegal to photocopy music.*

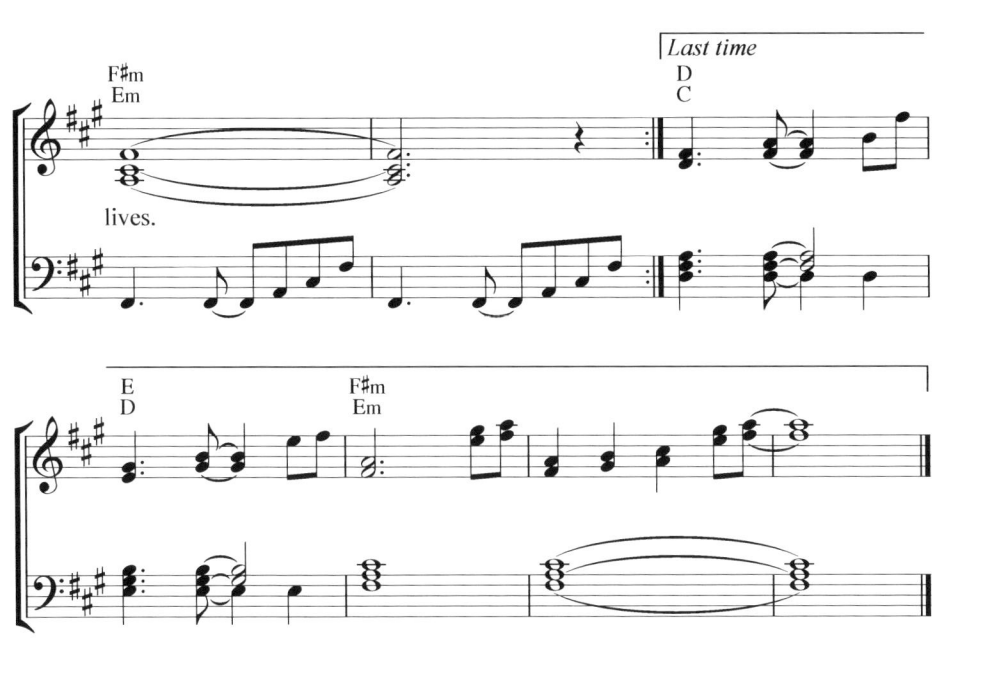

2. If there's rhythm, then let us clap it.
   If there's oscillation, let us swing it.
   If there's a purpose, then let us find it.
   Beating the Tango of our lives.

3. Grace-full and holy, life-giving movement,
   strength moving boldly, flowing together.
   Tuned to the other, sensuous beauty.
   Dancing the Tango of our lives.

# 147 The universe was waiting

Michael Forster (b.1946) — Alan Rees (1941-2005)

DORE ABBEY 76 76 D

1. The universe was waiting in dark chaotic night, until the word was spoken: 'Let there be glorious light!' From darkness and from chaos were light and order born; the God of new beginnings rejoiced to see their dawn.

© Copyright 1999 Kevin Mayhew Ltd.
*It is illegal to photocopy music.*

2. And as in that beginning,
   in ev'ry age the same,
   creation's Re-creator
   is keeping hope aflame.
   From Eden to the desert,
   the manger to the tomb,
   each fall becomes a rising,
   and ev'ry grave a womb.

3. Wherever people languish
   in darkness or despair,
   the God of new beginnings
   suffers and rises there.
   We join with him, to listen,
   to care, and to protest,
   to see the mighty humbled
   and all the humble blessed.

4. We join with our Creator
   to keep the vision bright:
   in places of oppression
   we call for freedom's light:
   a glorious new beginning,
   a universe at peace,
   where justice flows like fountains
   and praises never cease.

# 148 There's a long way

Barbara Glasson

Rod Boucher
arr. Marian Heller

**Jogging**

1. There's a long way be-tween here and heav-en if you tra-vel a-lone or at night. *Refrain* But the gap be-tween hea-ven and here has been breached, and the bridge has been crossed, so be bold-er. The

© Copyright 2015 Kevin Mayhew Ltd.
*It is illegal to photocopy music.*

2. There's a fine line between here and heaven
   if the dazzle in eyes blinds your sight.

3. There's a brave call between here and heaven
   if your courage takes you beyond fright.

4. There's a steep path between here and heaven
   if you're climbing uphill to starlight.

# 149 There's a time coming nearer

Susie Hare

Susie Hare (b.1947)

**Bright but steady**

1. There's a time coming nearer that the world waits to see, there's a power that's moving to take victory, there's a new expectation of the forthcoming days;

(2.) rides on the heavens and he shines like the sun, when the trumpet has sounded and the battle is won, Satan's armies will perish and his strongholds will fall

(3.) justice shall triumph over darkness and sin and a harvest of nations shall be gathered in; then the whole of creation will be held in his hand

© Copyright 2001 Kevin Mayhew Ltd.
*It is illegal to photocopy music.*

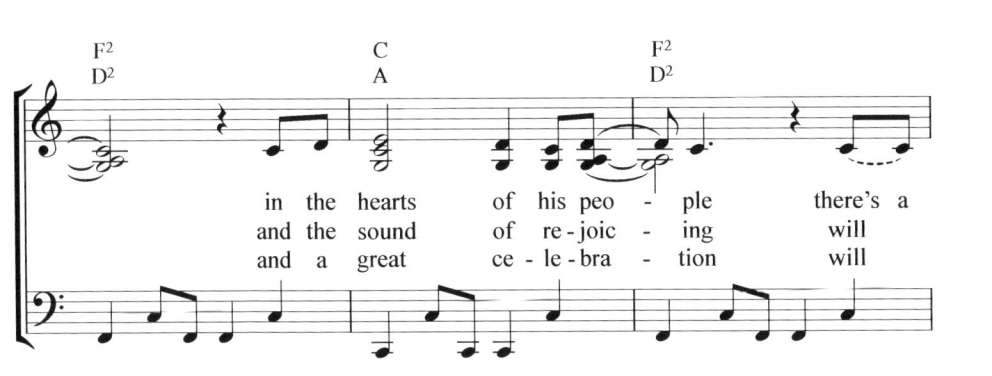

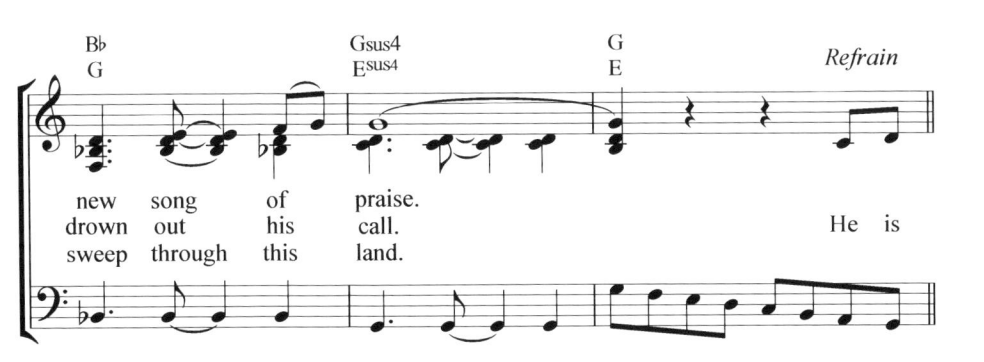

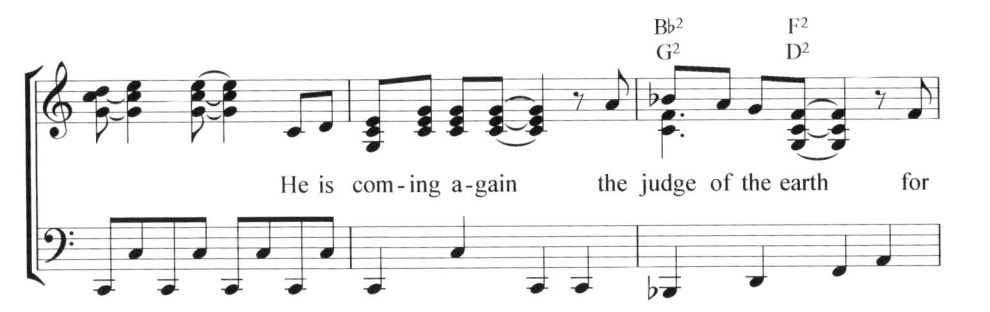

in the hearts of his peo - ple there's a
and the sound of re - joic - ing will
and a great ce - le - bra - tion will

new song of praise.
drown out his call.
sweep through this land. He is

*Refrain*

com - ing a - gain the judge of the earth for e - ver to reign.

He is com - ing a - gain the judge of the earth for

C Csus4 C G/B Am G
A Asus4 A E/G♯ F♯m E
e - ver to reign. Pre - pare the way,
F2 Am G F2
D2 F♯m E D2
pre - pare the way,
Am G F G C
F♯m E D E A
pre - pare the way, of the Lord.
Csus4 C G/B Am G F2
Asus4 A E/G♯ F♯m E D2
Pre - pare the way,

Am G F2 Am G
F#m E D2 F#m E
pre - pare the way, pre - pare the way,
F G C
D E A
1, 2.
of the Lord.
3.
D.S.
C
A
2. When he
3. Hea - ven's

## 150 Thirsty for the living water

Basil Bridge  Basil Bridge (b.1927)

LIVING WATER 87 833

1. Thirsty for the living water, hungry for the living bread, we in faith approach the table you have spread, gracious Lord.

2. Though your word and Spirit cleansed us,
   travel-stained your people meet;
   here you kneel with towel and basin
   at our feet,
   servant Lord.

3. We have heard your new commandment;
   you have shown us how to live;
   loved, we too would love; forgiven
   we forgive,
   loving Lord.

4. You see through us, know our weakness,
   hear the pray'rs and vows we make,
   grieve as we forget, disown you,
   and forsake,
   patient Lord.

5. You go with us as we travel,
   living truth, unfailing friend,
   light to guide and way to follow
   to the end,
   risen Lord.

© Copyright 2000 Kevin Mayhew Ltd.
*It is illegal to photocopy music.*

# 151 This heavenly love

Sean Bowman (1943-2013)  Geoffrey Nobes (b.1954)

1. This heav'n-ly love brings life, new life to fill the world, a life that gives to all we meet, a life that makes our lives com-plete. This heav'n-ly love brings life, new life to fill the world.

2. This heav'nly love brings joy,
   new joy to light the world,
   a joy that shows in ev'ry face,
   a joy that shines in ev'ry place.
   This heav'nly love brings joy,
   new joy to light the world.

3. This heav'nly love brings hope,
   new hope to lift the world,
   a hope that raises when we fall,
   a hope that answers when we call.
   This heav'nly love brings hope,
   new hope to lift the world.

4. This heav'nly love brings peace,
   new peace to calm the world,
   a peace to stem our flowing tears,
   a peace to calm our inner fears.
   This heav'nly love brings peace,
   new peace to calm the world.

© Copyright 2014 Kevin Mayhew Ltd.
*It is illegal to photocopy music.*

# 152 This side of heaven

## Oh, what a day!

Susie Hare

Susie Hare (b.1947)

**Easy ragtime style**

1. This side of hea - ven we know just in part, but
2. This side of hea - ven the things he has done are
3. This side of hea - ven we're fix - ing our eyes on

then we will know with all of our heart; for
pro - mi - ses now of what is to come; he's
run - ning the race and win - ning the prize; for

© Copyright 2001 Kevin Mayhew Ltd.
*It is illegal to photocopy music.*

what is un-seen and what is un-known will
lead-ing us on-ward to all that is planned, when
we have been cho-sen and called by his grace, and

one day to trust-ing hearts be shown.
one day in glo-ry we shall stand. Oh, what a day,
one day we'll see him face to face.

oh, what a day it will be!

Oh, what a sight, oh, what a sight we will see!

E E/B E E/G#
Oh, what a song, oh, what a song we will sing
A E/B
when we spend e - ter - ni - ty
Last time to Coda
1, 2.
F#m/B E/B E B
wor - ship-ping Je - sus the King!
3.
E A/C# B/D# F#m/E
And no-thing we've earned can take
E A/C# B/D# E
us there; the truth of our faith is sure, and

A/C♯ B/D♯ F♯m/E E
on - ly by mer - cy will we share his
F♯m7 B D.S.
glo-ri-ous home for e - ver-more!
CODA
E E/G♯ A F♯7/A♯ E/B
When we spend e-ter - ni-ty
F♯m/B G♯m/B A/B B E
wor-ship-ping Je - sus the King!

# Songs for a Servant Church

# 153 Together we proclaim

Martin E. Leckebusch (b.1962)  
Robert Jones (b.1945)

LLANGATTOCK SM

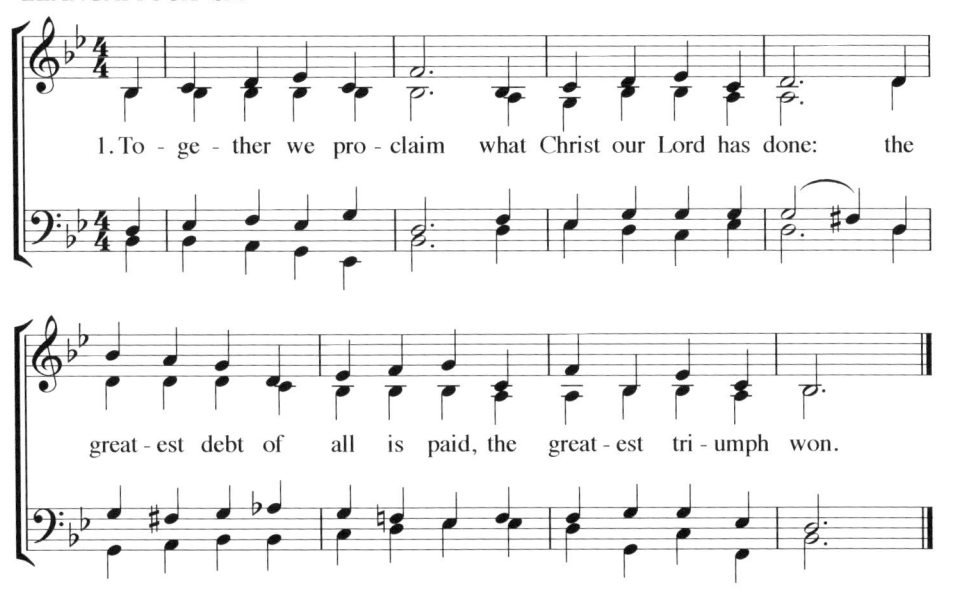

1. Together we proclaim what Christ our Lord has done: the greatest debt of all is paid, the greatest triumph won.

2. From anguished, straining pray'r
   to mocking robe and thorn
   to nails, a wooden cross and death
   our weight of guilt was borne.

3. One body, and one loaf —
   our hungry souls are fed;
   by faith we find the strength we need
   in Christ, the Living Bread.

4. The wine proclaims this truth:
   his life-blood sets us free
   to risk a life of faith and love,
   secure in liberty.

5. He gives us bread and wine
   and makes his life our own;
   renewed, we go, resolved afresh
   to make our Saviour known.

© Copyright 2000 Kevin Mayhew Ltd.  
*It is illegal to photocopy music.*

## 154 We have a vision

Jean Holloway (b.1939)　　　　　　　　　　　　　　　　　　　　Walter Greatorex (1877-1949)

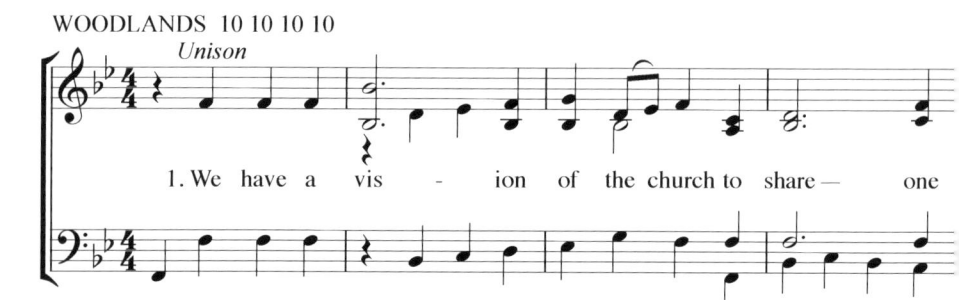

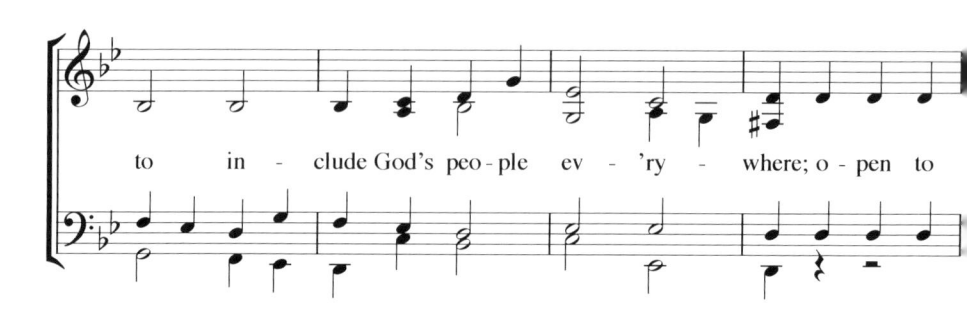

WOODLANDS 10 10 10 10

1. We have a vis-ion of the church to share — one to in-clude God's peo-ple ev-'ry-where; o-pen to all, and no one turned a-way, all those who en-ter here will wish to stay.

Text © Copyright 2000 Kevin Mayhew Ltd.
Music © reproduced by permission of Oxford University Press. All rights reserved.
*It is illegal to photocopy music.*

2. Here we embrace all people, young and old,
   welcoming those who come into our fold;
   holding the weak, encouraging the strong,
   each person valued, feeling they belong.

3. Gone is the fear of prejudice and hate —
   we seek to cherish, not humiliate;
   here we can own the failures that we know,
   firm in the faith that we can change and grow.

4. Humbly, we celebrate the good we do;
   testing the old, and trying out the new;
   using our talents, drawing on our skill,
   inspired by dreams and visions to fulfil.

5. Building upon the past that we hold dear,
   knowing tomorrow's task is still unclear;
   each step we take will help us on our way,
   one step will be sufficient for today.

6. Fired with the Spirit, filled with life and light,
   ours is a Church to challenge and excite;
   mission sustained by love and faith and prayer,
   extends God's love to people ev'rywhere.

# 155 We hear your cry, Lord

Garth Hewitt  Garth Hewitt

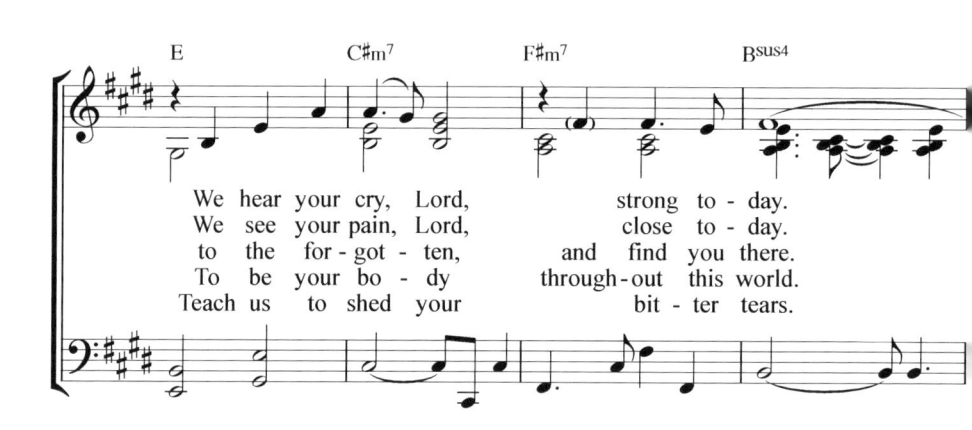

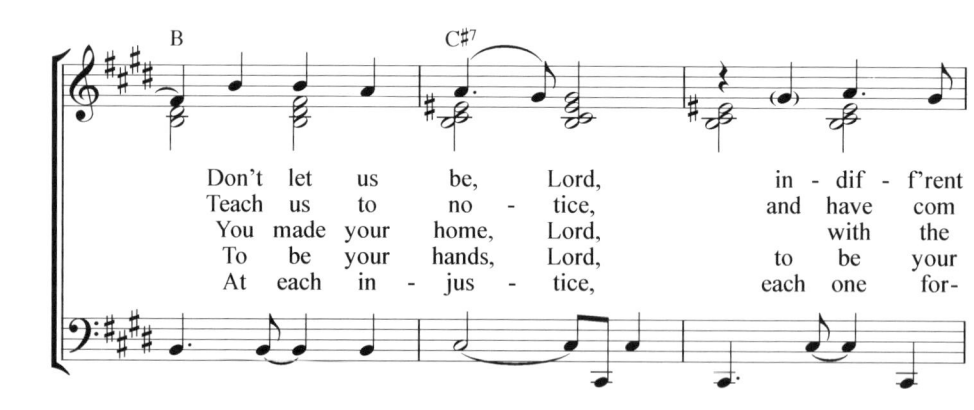

1. We hear your cry, Lord, in the hungry.
   We hear your cry, Lord, strong today.
   Don't let us be, Lord, indifferent

2. We see your pain, Lord, in the wounded.
   We see your pain, Lord, close today.
   Teach us to notice, and have com[passion]

3. Where you are lost, teach us to look, Lord,
   to the forgotten, and find you there.
   You made your home, Lord, with the

4. This is the task, Lord, that you have set us.
   To be your body throughout this world.
   To be your hands, Lord, to be your

5. We hear your cry, Lord, in the hungry.
   Teach us to shed your bitter tears.
   At each injustice, each one for-

© Copyright 2012 Kevin Mayhew Ltd.
*It is illegal to photocopy music.*

F♯m
Bsus4
to you; we hear your cry, Lord,
pas - sion; we see your face, Lord,
weak - est; teach us to fol - low,
feet, Lord; to have your heart, Lord,
got - ten; teach us to fol - low
B
E
A
E
E/G♯
help us o - bey. 2. We see your
a - mong the pain. 3. When we have
and find you there. 4. There is a
help us o - bey. 5. We hear your
and find you there, teach us to
F♯m
A/B
B
E
A/E
E
fol - low, and find you there.

## 156 We owe our thanks to you, Lord

Martin E. Leckebusch (b.1962) — Kevin Mayhew (b.1942)

HITCHAM 76 76 D

1. We owe our thanks to you, Lord — how lavishly you give! And how we love your presence — where better could we live? Yet all our finest worship can never clear our debt for pray'rs that you remember, for sins that you for-

© Copyright 2013 Kevin Mayhew Ltd.
It is illegal to photocopy music.

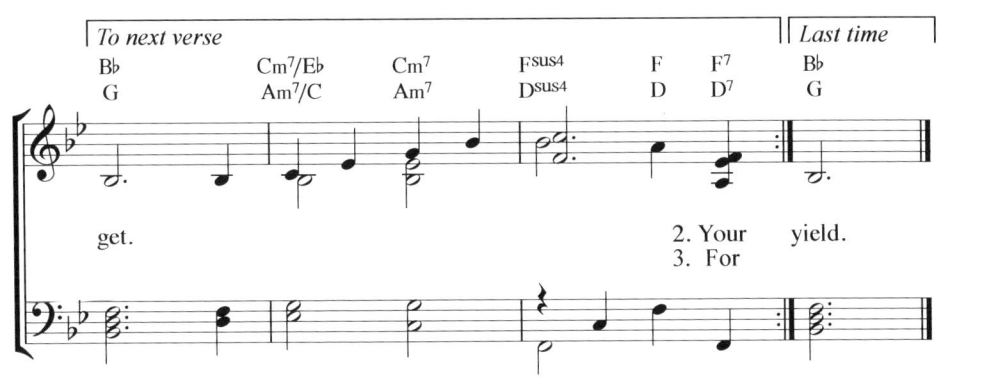

2. Your might is awe-inspiring,
   too vast for words to tell:
   what lofty peaks you fashion,
   what surging seas you quell!
   Your word commands the nations
   to spurn their evil ways,
   till those who see your wonders
   respond with rev'rent praise.

3. For nature's steady rhythms
   with all that they provide,
   for each abundant harvest
   and tables well-supplied,
   we join the thankful chorus
   of forest, hill and field
   to honour you, the Giver,
   for all creation's yield.

# 157 We remember you

Barbara Glasson

Rod Boucher
arr. Marian Hellen

**Exuberantly**

*Refrain*

We remember you. We remember you.

*Last time to Coda*

Your glory. Your wonder. Your promise.

1. The barley and the flax bow heads to the vesper, the harebell and dock laugh gently,

© Copyright 2015 Kevin Mayhew Ltd.
*It is illegal to photocopy music.*

2. The snowdrop and the dew declare to the night air,
   the cowslip and grass nod softly,
   the woodwind of branches respond with a fanfare:

3. The granite and the grit are drenched by the downpour,
   the bramble and briar sing firmly,
   the swift and the swallow will dance to the encore:

4. The elder and the larch wave leaves to the wide skies,
   the willow and birch rise proudly,
   the thrush and the fieldfare announce to the sunrise:

# 158 We saw beauty in the ashes — *Broken image*

Garth Hewitt  
Garth Hewitt

(♩ = 100)

1. We saw beau-ty in the ash-es, we saw trea-sure in the dust. We saw joy come out of mourn-ing, we saw dia-monds in the rough. And though the im-age may look bro-ken, we saw Je-sus shin-ing through and on each for-got-ten fea-ture he was writ-ing 'I love

© Copyright 2012 Kevin Mayhew Ltd.  
*It is illegal to photocopy music.*

*Refrain*
you.' Come and stand with the broken, come and learn from the poor. Take the side of those forgotten, let the image be restored. 2. As the stored.

2. As the poverty of riches leaves us stranded on the shore,
   where the rising tide of selfishness will leave us thirsty evermore.
   Our image of those in poverty must be broken once for all;
   to see the beauty in their lives, to hear the good news from the poor.

3. Come and walk the road with Jesus, on the side of the oppressed,
   come and stand inside the kingdom where the story is redressed.
   And though our image looks so broken, Jesus still says 'Follow me',
   and give yourself for others, and live in simplicity.

# 159 We will pray for you, sister

Garth Hewitt  
Garth Hewitt

1. We will pray for you, sister, we will pray for you, brother.

Down on our knees to show we love one an-o-ther, we will

*Last time to Coda*

*To next verse* | *Middle section - after v.3*

pray, pray, pray. 2. We will work. And to

those who much is giv-en, so much will be re-

© Copyright 2012 Kevin Mayhew Ltd.
*It is illegal to photocopy music.*

2. We will listen to you, sister,
   we will listen to you, brother.
   We will listen and learn to show
   we love one another.
   May we hear, hear, hear.

3. We will work for you, sister,
   we will work for you, brother.
   We will work all we can to show
   we love one another.
   We will work, work, work.

4. We will give for you, sister,
   we will give for you, brother.
   We will give all we can to show
   we love one another.
   We will give, give, give.

5. We will stand with you, sister,
   we will stand with you, brother.
   Stand arm in arm to show
   we love one another,
   we will stand, stand, stand.

6. Will you pray for me, sister,
   will you pray for me, brother?
   Down on your knees to show
   we love one another.
   Will you pray, pray, pray?
   Will you pray, pray, pray?

# 160 We've silenced our prophets     *Let justice roll*

Garth Hewitt                                                    Garth Hewitt

(♩ = 135)

1. We've si-lenced our pro-phets, we've shot down our dream-ers. Our life blood is mo-ney, we're ex-ploit-ing the poor. Oh, the peo-ple of the west, they just love to in-vest in the

© Copyright 2012 Kevin Mayhew Ltd.
*It is illegal to photocopy music.*

sys-tem that keeps the poor world poor.

**1.** A
**2.** A *Refrain* D G
2. And we Let jus-tice roll on like a

D G D A
ri - ver, truth like a

G D G/D D A^sus4 A
ne - ver-fail - ing, e-ver-flow-ing stream. Then

D G D G
tears of rage will turn to laugh-ter

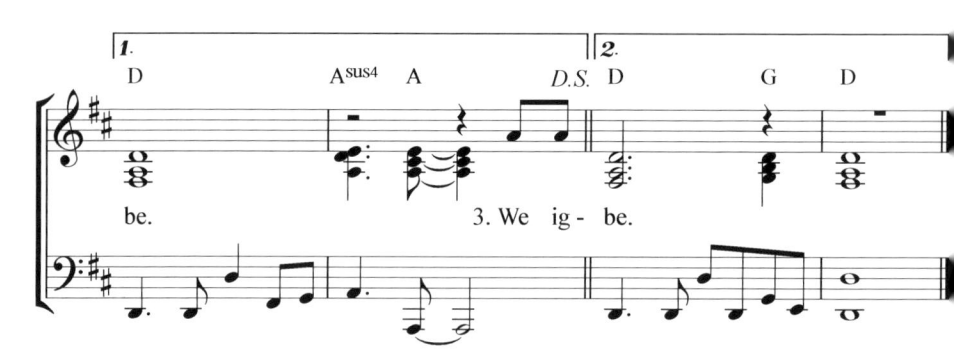

2. And we have no compassion,
   our lifestyle is evil.
   Higher living standards,
   that's the god we adore.
   Oh, the people of the west . . .

3. We ignore the ways of justice,
   though we talk a lot about it.
   We victimise the stranger
   seeking refuge in our land.
   Oh, the people of the west . . .

4. And greed is our mother,
   silence is our father.
   Our epitaph is written
   in frustrated tears of rage.
   Oh, the people of the west . . .

*Songs for a*
SERVANT
CHURCH

## 161 What a night to remember

Martin E. Leckebusch (b.1962)

Traditional English melody
arr. Donald Thomson

STOWEY 11 11 11 11

1. What a night to re-mem-ber, the words that Christ spoke, and the wine that he shared, and the bread that he broke! The suff'ring and glory to come were displayed, but his friends could not grasp he would soon be betrayed.

Text © Copyright 2010, and this music arrangement
© Copyright 2014 Kevin Mayhew Ltd.
*It is illegal to photocopy music.*

2. And of all nights this, surely, was one to forget,
   where companionship, failure and treachery met.
   In friendship Christ offered the wine and the bread —
   but when he was arrested, how swiftly they fled!

3. Yet he bids us remember, and tells us to think
   of his deeds as we eat, of his love as we drink:
   this feast for our souls brings a welcome release
   from the hunger for pardon, the thirst to find peace.

4. So we come in contrition; our hearts are exposed;
   and the road leading home to God's love is disclosed.
   The bread and the wine tell us: this is the place
   where our guilt is excised by the sharp edge of grace.

## 162 What can we say?

Barbara Glasson

Rod Boucher
arr. Marian Heller

**Forceful yet reflective**

1. What can we say, when words feel as load-ed as guns? Let's leave our shoes at the thresh-old, and touch our hands to our hearts. Dis-arm our sus-pic-ion with hope.

*Refrain*

Sa-

© Copyright 2015 Kevin Mayhew Ltd.
*It is illegal to photocopy music.*

2. How can we smile, our face seems as veiled as the truth?
   Let's leave our fear at the threshold
   and touch our hands to our hearts.
   Uncover a friendship of trust.

3. Whom can we touch, when heads wag like fingers of hate?
   Let's leave our doubt at the threshold
   and touch our hands to our hearts.
   Reach out in the name that is peace.

# 163 When the day grows cold

Michael Cockett (b.1938)        Kevin Mayhew (b.1942)

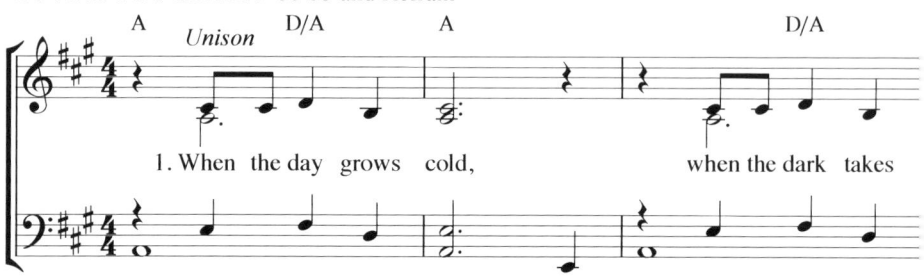

LOVING YOU GENTLY 55 55 and Refrain

1. When the day grows cold, when the dark takes hold, then I hear you say, 'Hope will light your way.'

*Refrain*
Loving you gently, Lord, knowing you're there, finding my faith in you, hope peace

© Copyright 1976 Kevin Mayhew Ltd.
*It is illegal to photocopy music.*

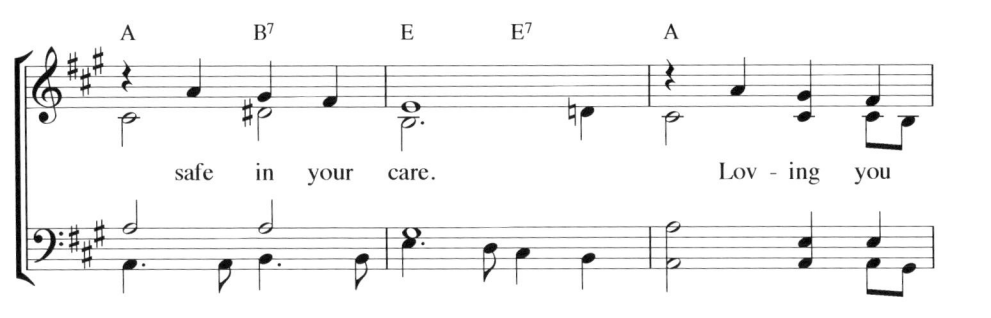

2. When the petals fall,
   when the winter calls,
   then I think of you,
   faith will rise anew.

3. When the gale has blown,
   when the storm has torn,
   then the calm recalls
   peace that conquers all.

## 164 When we were little, hurt and lost
### *Mothers of the world*

Lucy Berry (b.1957)          John Bacchus Dykes (1823-1876)

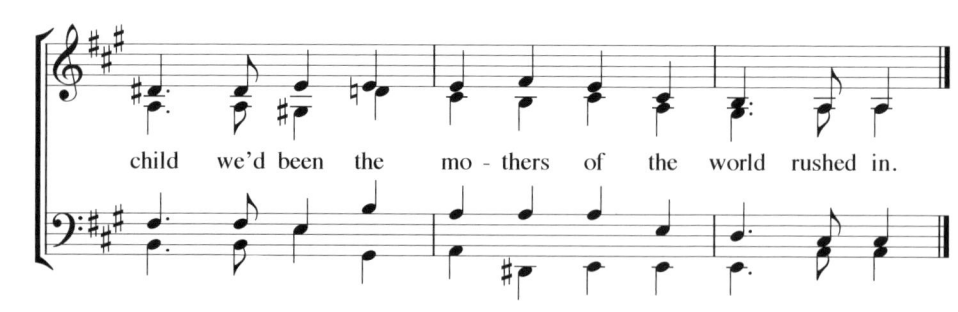

MELITA 88 88 88

1. When we were little, hurt and lost, or in some kind of trouble tossed and needed hands to soothe the pain and settle us to sleep again; whatever kind of child we'd been the mothers of the world rushed in.

Text © Copyright 2014 Kevin Mayhew Ltd.
*It is illegal to photocopy music.*

2. And when, grown up to adulthood,
   a chaos barely understood,
   sweeps in to smash and wound and burn
   so we can find no place to turn;
   however foolish we have been,
   the mothers of the world rush in:

3. Brave men and women come to fight
   our flames, our fears, our dreadest night,
   as rocks to our uncertainty,
   and servants to emergency.
   Through war and crime, through hurt and sin
   the mothers of the world rush in.

4. No wonder: all about the world
   the everlasting arms are curled
   of Holy Spirit, Jesus, God,
   to hold us through all fire, all flood.
   Whatever nightmare we have seen
   the mothers of the world rush in.

# 165 Where love is met with hatred

Nick Fawcett (b.1957)  Samuel Sebastian Wesley (1810-1876)

AURELIA 76 76 D

1. Where love is met with hat-red, and dreams have been snuffed out, where days are full of suff-'ring and faith has turned to doubt, where e-vil con-quers good-ness and life is full of care, grant through it all the know-ledge that you, O Lord, are there.

Text © Copyright 2006 Kevin Mayhew Ltd.
*It is illegal to photocopy music.*

2. Where joy has turned to sorrow
and hope gives way to fear,
where peace is cruelly shattered
as sudden storms appear,
where life belies convictions
on which we once relied,
grant through it all the knowledge
you're always by our side.

3. Where darkness like a shadow
extinguishes the light,
where plans are brought to ruin
and nothing quite goes right,
where health begins to falter
and life begins to fade,
grant through it all the knowledge
we need not be afraid.

4. To those enduring trouble
with which they cannot cope,
to those for whom disaster
has put an end to hope,
to those who carry burdens
too difficult to bear,
grant through it all the knowledge
that you, O Lord, are there.

# 166 Where you're going I will follow

Barbara Glasson

Rod Boucher
arr. Marian Hellen

**Rolling**

1. Where you're going, I will follow, I am certain of direction. In denial, I'm in shadow later on, in the everlasting rhythm of aloneness and connection.

*Refrain*
In the taking of the road, in the

walk-ing on the wa-ter, doubts and dreams and end-less dou-ble-binds.

Oh.  2. Can I

*Last time*

2. Can I wash my hands of trouble,
   remain doubtless in decisions,
   then to follow with my heart
   and conscience free,
   in the choices that seem fickle
   and the multiple corrections.

3. Seeing you there, standing waiting
   on the shoreline of our vision,
   with the fishes that we longed for
   all night long,
   in the promise of a breakfast
   at the fire of resurrection.

4. So if only you were walking
   to the final destination,
   solving questions that are hanging
   now you've gone.
   In your strangeness and your friendship
   is the gift of contradiction.

# 167 Within the busy rush of life

Martin E. Leckebusch (b.1962)          Malcolm Archer (b.1952)

KINGDOM 86 86 86

1. Within the busy rush of life I find a resting-place: when I submit to Christ my Lord and let him set my pace he shows the way that I should take whatever trials I face.

© Copyright 1999 Kevin Mayhew Ltd.
*It is illegal to photocopy music.*

2. Amid the choices I must make
   and duties that increase
   he comes to calm my anxious thoughts,
   to make the turmoil cease;
   as in his presence I remain
   he guides me into peace.

3. The timeless, all-sufficient God
   my ev'ry longing knows
   and daily he refreshes me
   with joy which overflows;
   anointed by tranquility,
   my strength to serve him grows.

4. My Saviour bids me walk with him
   and follow all his ways —
   his plan for me is fruitfulness
   throughout my earthly days,
   since now and evermore I live
   beneath his loving gaze.

# 168 You are the Bread of Life

Martin E. Leckebusch (b.1962)           Malcolm Archer (b.1953)

COURT BARTON DSM

1. You are the Bread of Life which feeds the hungry soul; your body, broken on the cross, was torn to make us whole. Your flesh is food so real, your blood is drink indeed — Lord Jesus, in your life we find the nourishment we need.

Text © Copyright 2000, and Music © Copyright 1999 Kevin Mayhew Ltd.
*It is illegal to photocopy music.*

2. You are the Prince of Peace,
   the one who offers rest
   for troubled, weary, aching hearts
   by burdens long oppressed.
   You will not weigh us down,
   our load you humbly bear —
   how glad we are to learn your ways,
   your easy yoke to share.

3. You are the only Way,
   the Truth whom we believe,
   and those who place their trust in you
   eternal life receive.
   You make the Father known,
   his glory lights your face —
   his splendour you reveal to us
   in mercy, truth and grace.

# 169 You've called us as your Church, Lord

Nick Fawcett (b.1957)  John Richardson (1816-1879)

VAUGHAN 76 76 D and Refrain

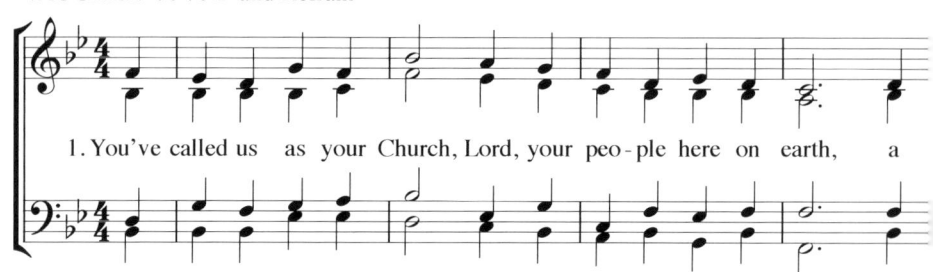

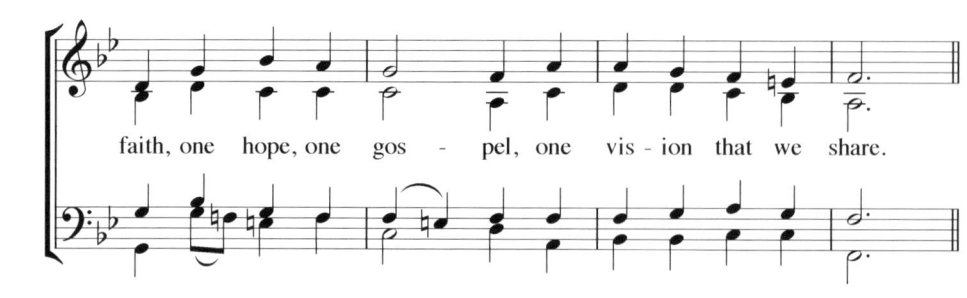

1. You've called us as your Church, Lord, your people here on earth, a fellowship of equals where all are given worth, a family together, distinguished by our care, one faith, one hope, one gospel, one vision that we share.

Text © Copyright 2006 Kevin Mayhew Ltd.
*It is illegal to photocopy music.*

*Refrain*

May cords of love unite us, too strong to be undone — although we may be many, equip us to be one.

2. Yet we have been divided
by doctrine, dogma, creed,
estranged from one another —
we've left your wounds to bleed.
Too full of our convictions,
believing others wrong,
we've lost sight of the body
to which we all belong.

3. Our diff'rences deny you,
betray the faith we claim;
instead of love uniting,
we squabble in your name.
Lord, heal the wounds that scar us —
suspicion, fear and pride;
reveal the good in others
that all our labels hide.

# Songs for a Servant Church

## INDEXES

**Index of Composers and Sources of Music**

**Index of Authors**

**Metrical Index of Tunes**

**Scriptural Index**

**Index of uses**

**Index of first lines and titles**

# INDEX OF COMPOSERS AND SOURCES OF MUSIC

| | |
|---|---|
| Archer, Malcolm | 6, 47, 49, 54, 66, 85, 88, 117, 167, 168 |
| Bach, Johann Sebastian | 57 |
| Bain, Brother James Macbeth | 139 |
| Beaumont, Geoffrey | 144 |
| Beethoven, Ludwig van | 9, 18 |
| Bishop, Henry R | 70 |
| Boucher, Rod | 8, 28, 48, 55, 73, 87, 89, 118, 127, 141, 146, 148, 157, 162, 166 |
| Brackett, Joseph | 128 |
| Bridge, Basil | 150 |
| Brierley, Michael | 72 |
| Converse, Charles Crozat | 75, 130 |
| Croatian folk melody | 90 |
| Crüger, Johann | 71 |
| Damon, William | 1 |
| Darwall, John | 2 |
| Dearle, Edward | 23 |
| Dekker, Thomas | 86 |
| Dykes, John Bacchus | 108, 164 |
| Elgar, Edward | 44, 67, 98 |
| Elliot, James William | 93 |
| 'Geistliche Lieder', Wittenberg | 42 |
| 'Gesangbuch', Johann Crüger | 71 |
| Greatorex, Walter | 154 |
| Grinnell, Andrew | 113 |
| Hand, Colin | 131 |
| Handel, George Frideric | 51, 131 |
| Hare, Susie | 17, 20, 24, 30, 37, 56, 59, 60, 61, 62, 63, 64, 76, 77, 78, 95, 97, 101, 102, 103, 114, 120, 121, 142, 149, 152 |
| Hassler, Hans Leo | 57 |
| Hawthorne, Val | 22 |
| Haydn, Franz Joseph | 90 |
| Hémy, Henri Friedrich | 25, 46, 58, 111, 112 |
| Hewitt, Garth | 10, 27, 52, 53, 65, 79, 83, 116, 134, 155, 158, 159, 160 |
| Higgins, Michael | 14 |
| Holst, Gustav | 68 |
| 'Hymn tunes of the United Brethren' | 84 |
| James, James | 81 |
| Jones, Robert | 153 |
| Kaihau, Maewa | 92, 106 |
| Kendrick, Graham | 123 |
| Maker, Frederick C. | 31 |
| Martin, George Clement | 39 |

| | |
|---|---|
| Mawby, Colin | 33, 139 |
| Mayhew, Kevin | 13, 38, 43, 94, 99, 105, 136, 137, 156, 163 |
| Monk, William Henry | 71 |
| Moore, Andrew | 19, 104, 129, 135 |
| 'Musikalisches Handbuch' | 15 |
| Nixon, June | 12, 40, 145 |
| Nobes, Geoffrey | 5, 11, 16, 26, 124, 126, 143, 151 |
| Parry, Charles Hubert Hastings | 4, 109 |
| Parry, Joseph | 41 |
| Petrus, Theodoricus | 36 |
| Plainsong melody | 104 |
| Plainsong melody (13th century) | 36 |
| Plainsong mode iii | 129 (Tune 1), 135 (Tune 1) |
| Rawsthorne, Noel | 96, 128, 133 |
| Rees, Alan | 7, 34, 147 |
| Richardson, John | 80, 169 |
| Ridout, Alan | 100, 132 |
| Roe, Betty | 125 |
| Root, George Frederick | 45 |
| Ross, Jane | 133 |
| Rowlands, William Penfro | 74 |
| Scot, Clement | 92, 106 |
| Stent, Keith | 119 |
| Stewart, Dorothy | 92, 106 |
| Tambling, Christopher | 9, 18, 82, 140 |
| Terry, Richard Runciman | 132 |
| 'The Psalmes in English Metre' | 1 |
| Thomson, Donald | 21, 44, 45, 50, 51, 67, 70, 81, 86, 98, 122, 128, 161 |
| Thrupp, Joseph Francis | 91 |
| 'Tochter Sion' | 29 |
| Traditional | 112 |
| Traditional Caribbean | 119 |
| Traditional English melody | 21, 69, 115, 161 |
| Traditional French melody | 122, 135 (Tune 2) |
| Traditional Irish melody | 133, 140 |
| Vaughan Williams, Ralph | 69, 115 |
| Watts, Sarah | 92, 106 |
| Webb, George James | 138 |
| Webbe, Samuel | 32, 107, 129 (Tune 2) |
| Wesley, Samuel Sebastian | 3, 35, 110, 165 |
| Wilkes, John Bernard | 84 |
| Wright, James | 50 |

# INDEX OF AUTHORS

| | |
|---|---|
| Berry, Jan | 19, 88 |
| Berry, Lucy | 15, 35, 47, 72, 84, 107, 164 |
| Bowman, Sean | 5, 11, 143, 151 |
| Bridge, Basil | 49, 74, 109, 150 |
| Cockett, Michael | 163 |
| Dainty, Peter | 124 |
| Fawcett, Nick | 3, 14, 26, 31, 40, 43, 45, 54, 57, 70, 86, 92 |
| | 95, 96, 98, 99, 102, 106, 125, 131, 165, 169 |
| Forster, Michael | 4, 7, 21, 42, 46, 68, 75, 81, 82, 100, 104, 110 |
| | 111, 112, 128, 130, 132, 145, 147 |
| Glasson, Barbara | 8, 28, 48, 55, 73, 87, 89, 118, 127, 141, 146, 148, 157, 162, 166 |
| Grinnell, Andrew | 113 |
| Hare, Susie | 17, 24, 30, 37, 56, 59, 60, 61, 62, 63, 64, 76, 77, 97, |
| | 101, 103, 114, 120, 121, 142, 149, 152 |
| Hawthorne, Val | 22 |
| Hewitt, Garth | 10, 27, 52, 53, 65, 79, 83, 116, 134, 155, 158, 159, 160 |
| Holloway, Jean | 23, 29, 33, 34, 44, 71, 93, 108, 154 |
| Jennens, Charles | 51 |
| Leckebusch, Martin | 1, 6, 9, 12, 13, 16, 18, 20, 25, 32, 38, 39, 41, 58, 67, 69, |
| | 78, 80, 85, 90, 91, 94, 115, 117, 122, 123, 133, 136, |
| | 137, 138, 139, 140, 144, 153, 156, 161, 167, 168 |
| Le Grice, Edwin | 2, 66 |
| Massey, Christopher | 36, 119, 129, 135 |
| Mayhew, Kevin | 105 |
| Nobes, Geoffrey | 126 |
| Wright, James | 50 |

# METRICAL INDEX OF TUNES

**CM**
Breathe in me 11
Brother James' Air 139
St Bernard 29
Thorpe Morieux 94

**DCM**
Forest Green 115
Monks Eleigh 137

**DLM**
Jerusalem 4

**DSM**
Court Barton 47, 168

**LM**
Church Triumphant 93
Farringdon 76
Golden slumbers 86
Melcombe 32, 107
Te lucis 104
Winchester New 15

**SM**
Llangattock 153
Southwell (Damon) 1

**55 55 and Refrain**
Loving you gently 163

**55 55 65 65**
St Kilda 145

**65 65 D**
Camberwell 72
Kelfield 125
Passion Chorale 57
Vicars' Close 54

**66 12 4 12**
Darwall's 148th 2

**66 66 44 44**
Open our eyes 117

**67 67 66 66**
Gracias 144

**75 75 777 7**
Froyle 30

**76 76 D**
Aurelia 3, 35, 110, 165
Crüger 71
Dore Abbey 147
Hitcham 156
Home sweet home 70
Morning light 138
Salley Gardens 140
Turris Davidica 25, 111

**76 76 D and Refrain**
Vaughan 169

**76 76 76 D**
Vaughan 80

**76 86 86 86**
St Christopher 31

**77 and Refrain**
Monkland 84

**77 76**
Jesus came to save us 124

**77 77 D**
Aberystwyth 41

**77 11 77 11 and Refrain**
Tramp! Tramp! Tramp! 45

**84 84 88 87 and Refrain**
Wonderful, glorious day! 121

**86 86 D**
Iver 58

**86 86 6**
Repton 109

**86 86 86**
Kingdom 167

**86 86 86 and Refrain**
God rest you merry 21

**86 86 86 866**
Powntley 114

**86 96 and Refrain**
Felsham 105

**86 96 96 87 and Refrain**
For I can do all things 61

**87 85**
Christ my teacher 16

**87 87**
Heavenly splendour 6, 66
Sussex 69

**87 833**
Living water 150

**87 87 67**
Mansfield 33

**87 87 77**
Black Madonna 100

**87 87 87**
| | |
|---|---|
| Gouldsbrook | 49 |
| Pange lingua | 129(i), 135(i) |
| Sacrum convivium | 7 |
| St Helen | 39 |
| St Thomas (Webbe) | 129(ii) |
| Tantum ergo (Grafton) | 135(ii) |

**87 87 D**
| | |
|---|---|
| Austria | 90 |
| Ave Verum | 44, 67 |
| Blaenwern | 74 |
| Brettenham | 43 |
| Castlemaine | 40 |
| Kersey | 13 |
| Melford | 95 |
| Ode to joy | 9, 18 |
| Odiham | 78 |
| Quinton | 64 |
| Tor Hill | 88 |
| What a friend (Converse) | 75, 130 |
| Willaston | 96 |

**87 87 D and Refrain**
| | |
|---|---|
| Runciman | 132 |

**87 87 8 87**
| | |
|---|---|
| Luther | 42 |

**87 87 87 7**
| | |
|---|---|
| Corde natus (Divinum mysterium) | 36 |

**87 98 87**
| | |
|---|---|
| Besançon Carol | 122 |

**88 10 10**
| | |
|---|---|
| Mother of Christ | 102 |

**88 88 D**
| | |
|---|---|
| Multicoloured tapestry | 136 |

**88 88 88**
| | |
|---|---|
| Eastrop | 20 |
| Melita | 108, 164 |
| St Catherine (Tynemouth) | 46 |
| Stella | 112 |

**89 98**
| | |
|---|---|
| Cosford | 14 |

**9 10 10 9 10 10 10 extended**
| | |
|---|---|
| Rattlesden | 38 |

**9 10 10 10**
| | |
|---|---|
| Hallelujah | 26 |

**10 10 10 4 and Alleluias**
| | |
|---|---|
| Stogursey | 85 |

**10 10 10 10**
| | |
|---|---|
| Ad limina | 19 |
| Buxhall | 99 |
| Penitentia | 23 |
| Woodlands | 154 |

**10 66 10 8**
| | |
|---|---|
| Handel | 131 |

**11 10 11 10**
| | |
|---|---|
| At this day's end | 5 |
| Epiphany | 91 |

**11 10 11 10 11 10 11 12**
| | |
|---|---|
| Danny Boy | 133 |

**11 11 11 6**
| | |
|---|---|
| Salut d'amour | 98 |

**11 11 11 8 and Refrain**
| | |
|---|---|
| Land of my fathers | 81 |

**11 11 11 11**
| | |
|---|---|
| Stowey | 161 |

**12 12 12 10 and Refrain**
| | |
|---|---|
| Simple gifts | 128 |

**13 13 13 13 13 13**
| | |
|---|---|
| Thaxted | 68 |

# SCRIPTURAL INDEX

## Genesis
| | | |
|---|---|---|
| 1:1-5 | God is our strength | 42 |
| | From the heart of God the Father | 36 |
| 1:1-19 | Let all creation's wonders | 80 |
| 1:3 | The universe was waiting | 147 |
| 1:26 | Living God, your word has called us | 88 |
| 2:7 | Breathe in me, Lord | 11 |
| 2:8 | In the peace of a garden | 70 |
| 3:1-24 | In the peace of a garden | 70 |

## Exodus
| | | |
|---|---|---|
| 25:4 | Living God, your word has called us | 88 |

## Deuteronomy
| | | |
|---|---|---|
| 7:9 | Don't be afraid | 22 |

## Psalms
| | | |
|---|---|---|
| 16 | God beyond earth's finest treasures | 39 |
| 26:7 | For riches of salvation | 30 |
| 36:6 | How rich and deep God's judgements are | 58 |
| 55:1-2 | Let all creation's wonders | 80 |
| 69:3 | For riches of salvation | 30 |
| 69:7 | Jesus, in your life we see you | 74 |
| 91 | Don't be afraid | 22 |
| 96 | Bring to God your new, best songs | 12 |
| 100 | All nations of the world | 2 |
| 100:4 | For riches of salvation | 30 |
| 121 | I lift my eyes to the hills | 60 |
| 148:1-13 | Let all creation's wonders | 80 |
| 150:6 | Let all creation's wonders | 80 |

## Amos
| | | |
|---|---|---|
| 5:24 | Justice like a river | 79 |
| | We've silenced our prophets | 160 |

## Isaiah
| | | |
|---|---|---|
| 2:4 | O God of hope | 109 |
| 12:2 | For riches of salvation | 30 |
| 25:4 | God is our strength | 42 |
| 42:6-7 | The Spirit of God | 145 |
| 53:3 | Praise to Christ, the Lord incarnate | 123 |
| 53:4-5 | If we have never sought Jesus, in your life we see you | 65 / 74 |
| 55:1 | Now, come to the water | 105 |
| 61:1-2 | The Spirit of God | 145 |
| 61:3 | The gracious invitation | 137 |

## Jeremiah
| | | |
|---|---|---|
| 14:8 | God is our strength | 42 |
| 17:13 | God is our strength | 42 |

## Lamentations
| | | |
|---|---|---|
| 3:23 | Lord, you have blessed me | 99 |

## Matthew
| | | |
|---|---|---|
| 1:18-25 | Good Joseph was a man | 47 |
| 1:21 | O West Bank town of Bethlehem | 115 |
| 2:1-12 | Light of her life | 86 |
| | The promised time arrives | 144 |
| 2:13-18 | In the night, the sound of crying | 69 |
| 2:13-23 | Good Joseph was a man | 47 |
| 3:3 | An urgent voice is calling | 3 |
| 4:16 | God is our strength | 42 |
| 5:3-12 | Feast your mind on what is pure | 27 |
| 5:13-16 | Called by Christ to be disciples | 13 |
| | Called to shed light | 14 |
| 6:9-13 | Lord Jesus, plant a seed of faith | 94 |
| | The day will come | 136 |
| | Our Father (Caribbean) | 119 |
| 9:10-12 | Jesus meets us at the margins | 75 |

**Matthew** continued
| | | |
|---|---|---|
| 9:35 | Jesus, in your life we see you | 74 |
| 10:7-8 | Called by Christ to be disciples | 13 |
| 10:37-39 | Jesus, we have heard your Spirit | 78 |
| 16:18 | Is the church a building? | 72 |
| 16:24-28 | Jesus, we have heard your Spirit | 78 |
| 25:29 | We will pray for you, sister | 159 |
| 25:31-46 | Be the hands of Jesus | 10 |
| | Teach us how to walk | 134 |
| 26:26-29 | At this table we remember | 6 |
| | What a night to remember | 161 |
| 26:36-45 | In the peace of a garden | 70 |
| | Now is the time | 106 |
| 27:26-50 | A crown of piercing thorns | 1 |
| 28:1-8 | In the peace of a garden | 70 |

**Mark**
| | | |
|---|---|---|
| 1:3 | An urgent voice is calling | 3 |
| 4:3-9 | Lord Jesus, plant a seed of faith | 94 |
| 5:25-28 | From a manger in a stable | 33 |
| 6:56 | From a manger in a stable | 33 |
| 8:34-38 | Jesus, we have heard your Spirit | 78 |
| 14:15 | Room prepared; disciples meet | 124 |
| 14:22-25 | At this table we remember | 6 |
| 15:15-37 | A crown of piercing thorns | 1 |
| 16:15 | Called by Christ to be disciples | 13 |

**Luke**
| | | |
|---|---|---|
| 1:26-38 | Fearful, uncertain | 26 |
| | Mary, blessèd teenage mother | 100 |
| | Mother of Christ, called from above | 102 |
| 2:1-20 | Hallelu, hallelu, hallelujah | 50 |
| | No gift so wonderful | 103 |
| 2:1-7 | Light of her life | 86 |
| | Mother of Christ, called from above | 102 |
| 2:7 | The promised time arrives | 144 |
| 2:13-14 | O West Bank town of Bethlehem | 115 |

| | | |
|---|---|---|
| 2:39-52 | Good Joseph was a man | 47 |
| 3:4 | An urgent voice is calling | 3 |
| 3:22 | God is our strength | 42 |
| 4:16-22 | The Spirit of God | 145 |
| 4:19 | Jesus, in your life we see you | 74 |
| 5:29-32 | Jesus meets us at the margins | 75 |
| 9:1-2 | Called by Christ to be disciples | 13 |
| 9:23-27 | Jesus, we have heard your Spirit | 78 |
| 11:2-4 | The day will come | 136 |
| | Our Father (Caribbean) | 119 |
| 14:15-24 | The gracious invitation | 137 |
| 15:1-10 | Jesus meets us at the margins | 75 |
| 15:11-31 | The gracious invitation | 137 |
| 22:12 | Room prepared; disciples meet | 124 |
| 22:14-20 | At this table we remember | 6 |
| 22:19-20 | What a night to remember | 161 |
| 24:13-32 | Sad, confused and shaken | 125 |

**John**
| | | |
|---|---|---|
| 1:1-14 | From the heart of God the Father | 36 |
| 1:14 | God is our strength | 42 |
| 1:16 | And can we hope | 4 |
| 2:1-10 | And can we hope | 4 |
| 3:2 | Christ, my teacher | 16 |
| 4:5-30 | He broke the rules | 53 |
| | Living water | 89 |
| 4:15 | Thirsty for living water | 150 |
| 5.23 | Give me a heart that will honour you | 38 |
| 6:32-35 | Feast your mind on what is pure | 27 |
| 13:1-15 | Room prepared; disciples meet | 124 |
| 13:4-15 | Image of our God and Father | 66 |
| 13:34-35 | Living God, your word has called us | 88 |
| 14:16 | The gracious invitation | 137 |
| 14:23-28 | What a night to remember | 161 |
| 16:24 | Room prepared; disciples meet | 124 |
| 19:1-2 | A crown of piercing thorns | 1 |

| | | |
|---|---|---|
| 19:34 | A crown of piercing thorns | 1 |
| 20:21 | Room prepared; disciples meet | 124 |
| 20:22 | Breathe in me, Lord | 11 |
| 21:4-19 | Where you're going I will follow | 166 |
| 21:19 | Sad, confused and shaken | 125 |

**Acts**

| | | |
|---|---|---|
| 20:29 | The day will come | 136 |

**Romans**

| | | |
|---|---|---|
| 8:14-17 | Jesus, we have heard your Spirit | 78 |

**Galatians**

| | | |
|---|---|---|
| 6:2 | Happy to share | 52 |

**Ephesians**

| | | |
|---|---|---|
| 4:3-6 | God of love | 44 |

**Philippians**

| | | |
|---|---|---|
| 2:6-9 | Image of our God and Father | 66 |
| 5:23 | Feast your mind on what is pure | 27 |

**Colossians**

| | | |
|---|---|---|
| 1:24 | Is the church a building? | 72 |

**James**

| | | |
|---|---|---|
| 1:17 | Lord Jesus, plant a seed of faith | 94 |

**I Peter**

| | | |
|---|---|---|
| 2:9-10 | Jesus, we have heard your Spirit | 78 |

**I John**

| | | |
|---|---|---|
| 1:1 | God is our strength | 42 |
| 1:8 | God is our strength | 42 |

**Revelation**

| | | |
|---|---|---|
| 1:8 | Every land in all creation | 24 |
| 1:11 | God of present, God of past | 45 |
| 2:4 | The day will come | 136 |
| 7:9-10 | Such a host as none can number | 132 |
| 19 | The heavens proclaim God's glory | 138 |
| 19:16 | Hallelujah | 51 |
| 21:6 | God is our strength | 42 |
| | God of present, God of past | 45 |
| 22:2 | In the peace of a garden | 70 |
| 22:13 | God is our strength | 42 |
| | God of present, God of past | 45 |

# INDEX OF USES

## GOD

### Creator / Creation
| | |
|---|---|
| All nations of the world | 2 |
| Bring to God your new, best songs | 12 |
| Creating God, we bring our songs of praise | 19 |
| Creation sings! | 20 |
| For beauty which delights our eyes | 29 |
| From the heart of God the Father | 36 |
| God is our strength | 42 |
| Gracious God, in adoration | 49 |
| I lift my eyes to the hills | 60 |
| I will always sing the praises | 64 |
| Let all creation's wonders | 80 |
| Mighty, magnificent God | 101 |
| The heavens proclaim God's glory | 138 |
| The Lord reveals his glory | 140 |
| The universe was waiting | 147 |
| We owe our thanks to you, Lord | 156 |

### Eternal life
| | |
|---|---|
| And can we hope | 4 |

### Godhead
| | |
|---|---|
| At your feet | 7 |
| Be the God of all my Sundays | 9 |
| Creating God, we bring our songs of praise | 19 |
| Extol the God of justice | 25 |
| From the heart of God the Father | 36 |
| God beyond earth's finest treasures | 39 |
| Gracious God, in adoration | 49 |
| How rich and deep God's judgements are | 58 |
| Sing 'Hey!' for the God who is eternally new | 128 |

### Faithfulness
| | |
|---|---|
| Don't be afraid | 22 |
| God of present, God of past | 45 |
| How amazing | 56 |
| I live, dependent on Jesus | 61 |
| I stand on a rock | 62 |
| Let us all, with grateful minds | 84 |
| Lord, you amaze us | 98 |
| Lord, you have blessed me | 99 |
| We owe our thanks to you, Lord | 156 |

### Father
| | |
|---|---|
| From the heart of God the Father | 36 |
| Our Father (Caribbean) | 119 |
| Our Father in heaven | 120 |

### Glory
| | |
|---|---|
| Every land in all creation | 24 |
| God beyond earth's finest treasures | 39 |
| God is our strength | 42 |
| God of life, we come in worship | 43 |
| Hallelujah | 51 |
| Sing 'Hey!' for the God who is eternally new | 128 |
| The Lord reveals his glory | 140 |

### Forgiveness and Mercy
| | |
|---|---|
| At this day's end | 5 |
| Christ, here we are! | 15 |
| Creating God, we bring our songs of praise | 19 |
| For riches of salvation | 30 |
| Forgive us when our deeds ignore | 32 |
| Good Lord, deliver us | 48 |
| I live, dependent on Jesus | 61 |
| I will always sing the praises | 64 |
| In the peace of a garden | 70 |
| Let us all, with grateful minds | 84 |
| Lord, you amaze us | 98 |
| Lord, you have blessed me | 99 |
| O Love that searches all my soul | 114 |
| The gracious invitation | 137 |
| The heavens proclaim God's glory | 138 |

## Grace
| | |
|---|---|
| Christ, here we are! | 15 |
| Feast your mind on what is pure | 27 |
| God of present, God of past | 45 |
| Humble yourselves | 59 |
| In the peace of a garden | 70 |
| Let love be our glory | 81 |
| Let us all, with grateful minds | 84 |
| Let us rejoice | 85 |
| Lord, you amaze us | 98 |
| Lord, you have blessed me | 99 |
| Now, come to the water | 105 |
| The man of the margins | 141 |

## Guidance
| | |
|---|---|
| Christ, my teacher | 16 |
| Jesus, we have heard your Spirit | 78 |

## Healing
| | |
|---|---|
| Come, rest in the love of Jesus | 17 |
| In an age of twisted values | 67 |
| Jesus shall reign | 76 |
| Lord, change our world | 92 |
| O God of thoughts and feelings | 110 |

## Jesus Christ
| | |
|---|---|
| A crown of piercing thorns | 1 |
| Be the hands of Jesus | 10 |
| Called by Christ to be disciples | 13 |
| Christ, here we are! | 15 |
| Christ, my teacher | 16 |
| Come, rest in the love of Jesus | 17 |
| From a manger in a stable | 33 |
| From opposite directions | 35 |
| From the heart of God the Father | 36 |
| From the heights of glory | 37 |
| God is our strength | 42 |
| God of love | 44 |
| Good Joseph was a man | 47 |
| Hallelu, hallelu, hallelujah | 50 |
| He broke the rules | 53 |
| How amazing | 56 |
| How did you feel, Lord Jesus | 57 |
| I was lost but now I'm found | 63 |
| I will always sing the praises | 64 |
| If we have never sought | 65 |
| Image of our God and Father | 66 |
| Jesus, in your life we see you | 74 |
| Jesus meets us at the margins | 75 |
| Jesus shall reign | 76 |
| Jesus, the Holy One | 77 |
| Light of her life | 86 |
| Lord Jesus, plant a seed of faith | 94 |
| Now is the time | 106 |
| One of us, flesh and blood | 116 |
| Out of the darkness of the night | 121 |
| People, look east | 122 |
| Praise to Christ, the Lord incarnate | 123 |
| Room prepared; disciples meet | 124 |
| The man of the margins | 141 |
| The only power that cleanses me | 142 |
| The promised time arrives | 144 |
| There's a long way | 148 |
| We saw beauty in the ashes | 158 |

## King and Kingdom
| | |
|---|---|
| Every land in all creation | 24 |
| Hallelujah | 51 |
| I live, dependent on Jesus | 61 |
| Jesus shall reign | 76 |
| Mighty, magnificent God | 101 |
| O holy, heavenly kingdom | 111 |

## Love
| | |
|---|---|
| And can we hope | 4 |
| Christ, here we are! | 15 |
| Come, rest in the love of Jesus | 17 |
| Don't be afraid | 22 |
| For riches of salvation | 30 |
| From opposite directions | 35 |
| From the heart of God the Father | 36 |
| God of life, we come in worship | 43 |
| God of love | 44 |
| He broke the rules | 53 |
| How amazing | 56 |
| I lift my eyes to the hills | 60 |
| Jesus, in your life we see you | 74 |
| Let love be our glory | 81 |
| Let love be real | 82 |
| Let us all, with grateful minds | 84 |
| Lord, what a sacrifice I see | 97 |
| Lord, you amaze us | 98 |
| Lord, you have blessed me | 99 |
| No gift so wonderful | 103 |
| O Father, on your love we call | 108 |
| O Lord, how long | 112 |

### Love continued
| | |
|---|---|
| O Love that searches all my soul | 114 |
| Sound out his praises | 131 |
| The Lord created family | 139 |
| This heavenly love brings life | 151 |
| We owe our thanks to you, Lord | 156 |
| We saw beauty in the ashes | 158 |

### Protector and provider
| | |
|---|---|
| At this day's end | 5 |
| Don't be afraid | 22 |
| I lift my eyes to the hills | 60 |
| Now, come to the water | 105 |
| We owe our thanks to you, Lord | 156 |
| When we were little, hurt and lost | 164 |

### Resurrection
| | |
|---|---|
| In the peace of a garden | 70 |
| Jesus, in your life we see you | 74 |
| Room prepared; disciples meet | 124 |

### Sacrificial and Atoning death
| | |
|---|---|
| A crown of piercing thorns | 1 |
| At this table we remember | 6 |
| From a manger in a stable | 33 |
| God has promised many things | 41 |
| I will always sing the praises | 64 |
| In the peace of a garden | 70 |
| Jesus, the Holy One | 77 |
| Lord, what a sacrifice I see | 97 |
| Now is the time | 106 |
| Room prepared; disciples meet | 124 |
| Sing, my tongue, the glorious struggle | 129 |
| Tell, my tongue, the awesome mystery | 135 |
| Together we proclaim | 153 |

### Saviour/Rescuer
| | |
|---|---|
| A crown of piercing thorns | 1 |
| God is our strength | 42 |
| Good Lord, deliver us | 48 |
| Saviour, precious Saviour | 126 |
| Sing, my tongue, the glorious struggle | 129 |
| Tell, my tongue, the awesome mystery | 135 |

### Spirit
| | |
|---|---|
| Breathe in me, Lord | 11 |
| God is our strength | 42 |
| God of love | 44 |
| Jesus, we have heard your Spirit | 78 |
| O Lord, how long | 112 |
| The Spirit of God | 145 |

### Trinity
| | |
|---|---|
| From the heart of God the Father | 36 |
| Image of our God and Father | 66 |

## CHURCH
### Faith Community
| | |
|---|---|
| Christ, here we are! | 15 |
| God of love | 44 |
| Is the church a building? | 72 |
| Let love be our glory | 81 |
| The day will come | 136 |
| The Lord created family | 139 |
| We have a vision | 154 |

### Listening Community
| | |
|---|---|
| From near and far | 34 |
| Listen up | 87 |

### Mission
| | |
|---|---|
| And can we hope | 4 |
| God of the nations | 46 |
| In an age of twisted values | 67 |
| Is the church a building? | 72 |
| Let love be our glory | 81 |
| O Lord, how long | 112 |

### Serving
| | |
|---|---|
| Be the hands of Jesus | 10 |
| God of love | 44 |
| Happy to share | 52 |
| In vast, ornate cathedrals | 71 |
| Is the church a building? | 72 |
| Let love be our glory | 81 |
| Let love be real | 82 |
| We have a vision | 154 |
| We hear your cry, Lord | 155 |
| We saw beauty in the ashes | 158 |
| We will pray for you, sister | 159 |

### Unity
| | |
|---|---|
| Be the hands of Jesus | 10 |
| From near and far | 34 |
| Living God, your word has called us | 88 |

### Welcoming
| | |
|---|---|
| Let the world be changed | 83 |
| Open the door | 118 |
| The day will come | 136 |
| The man of the margins | 141 |
| We have a vision | 154 |

### Witnessing in word and action
| | |
|---|---|
| Called by Christ to be disciples | 13 |
| From near and far | 34 |
| In vast, ornate cathedrals | 71 |
| Is the church a building? | 72 |
| Jesus, we have heard your spirit | 78 |
| O Lord, how long | 112 |
| The universe was waiting | 147 |
| We have a vision | 154 |

### Worshipping
| | |
|---|---|
| From near and far | 34 |
| God of life, we come in worship | 43 |
| God of love | 44 |
| In vast, ornate cathedrals | 71 |
| Is the church a building? | 72 |
| Jesus, the Holy One | 77 |
| Our Father in heaven | 120 |
| This side of heaven | 152 |

### Worldwide Community
| | |
|---|---|
| Every land in all creation | 24 |
| From near and far | 34 |
| Jesus shall reign | 76 |
| The day will come | 136 |
| We will pray for you, sister | 159 |

## JUSTICE
| | |
|---|---|
| An urgent voice is calling | 3 |
| And can we hope | 4 |
| Called by Christ to be disciples | 13 |
| Cry 'Freedom!' | 21 |
| Extol the God of justice | 25 |
| For those who strive for justice | 31 |
| From opposite directions | 35 |
| God of the nations | 46 |
| Good Lord, deliver us | 48 |
| Happy to share | 52 |
| In an age of twisted values | 67 |
| Jesus, we have heard your Spirit | 78 |
| Justice like a river | 79 |
| O God of hope | 109 |
| O Lord, how long | 112 |
| The day will come | 136 |
| We hear your cry, Lord | 155 |
| We saw beauty in the ashes | 158 |
| We've silenced our prophets | 160 |

## LIFE OF FAITH
### Alert
| | |
|---|---|
| Breathe in me, Lord | 11 |

### Assurance
| | |
|---|---|
| Don't be afraid | 22 |
| I live, dependent on Jesus | 61 |
| I stand on a rock | 62 |
| Let us all, with grateful minds | 84 |
| Lord, you amaze us | 98 |
| Lord, you have blessed me | 99 |
| O Lord, how long | 112 |
| The gracious invitation | 137 |

### Called
| | |
|---|---|
| Called by Christ to be disciples | 13 |
| Called to shed light | 14 |

### Comfort and Challenge
| | |
|---|---|
| Christ, my teacher | 16 |
| Come, rest in the love of Jesus | 17 |
| I lift my eyes to the hills | 60 |
| Is the church a building? | 72 |

### Commitment
| | |
|---|---|
| Be the God of all my Sundays | 9 |
| Called by Christ to be disciples | 13 |
| Called to shed light | 14 |
| Christ my teacher | 16 |
| Give me a heart that will honour you | 38 |
| God beyond earth's finest treasures | 39 |
| God of present, God of past | 45 |
| Good Joseph was a man | 47 |
| How rich and deep God's judgements are | 58 |
| In glad and sad remembrance | 68 |
| Jesus, we have heard your Spirit | 78 |
| Let love be our glory | 81 |
| Lord Jesus, plant a seed of faith | 94 |

## Commitment *continued*
| | |
|---|---|
| O Lord, how long | 112 |
| Set the sail on your boat | 127 |
| The path is stony | 143 |

## Confirmation
| | |
|---|---|
| Be the God of all my Sundays | 9 |

## Courage
| | |
|---|---|
| For riches of salvation | 30 |
| God of present, God of past | 45 |
| Let love be our glory | 81 |
| O God of thoughts and feelings | 110 |
| There's a long way | 148 |

## Discipleship
| | |
|---|---|
| Called by Christ to be disciples | 13 |
| Called to shed light | 14 |
| Christ, here we are! | 15 |
| Jesus, we have heard your Spirit | 78 |
| We hear your cry, Lord | 155 |
| We saw beauty in the ashes | 158 |
| Where you're going I will follow | 166 |

## Faith
| | |
|---|---|
| God has promised many things | 41 |
| Lord Jesus, plant a seed of faith | 94 |
| O God of thoughts and feelings | 110 |
| When the day grows cold | 163 |

## Freedom
| | |
|---|---|
| Finding a way | 28 |

## Hope
| | |
|---|---|
| And can we hope | 4 |
| Christ, here we are! | 15 |
| Finding a way | 28 |
| Living water | 89 |
| Lord Jesus, plant a seed of faith | 94 |
| O God of thoughts and feelings | 110 |
| This heavenly love brings life | 151 |
| When the day grows cold | 163 |

## Humility
| | |
|---|---|
| Humble yourselves | 59 |

## Love
| | |
|---|---|
| And can we hope | 4 |
| Come, rest in the love of Jesus | 17 |
| Let love be our glory | 81 |
| Let us all, with grateful minds | 84 |
| This heavenly love brings life | 151 |

## Peace
| | |
|---|---|
| Breathe in me, Lord | 11 |
| Come, rest in the love of Jesus | 17 |
| It's the morning after | 73 |
| Lord, you amaze us | 98 |
| The path is stony | 143 |
| This heaveny love brings life | 151 |
| When the day grows cold | 163 |
| Within the busy rush of life | 167 |

## Perseverance and Persistence
| | |
|---|---|
| God of present, God of past | 45 |
| Hold tight | 55 |
| Is the church a building? | 72 |

## Prayer
| | |
|---|---|
| Draw us together at the close of day | 23 |
| Give me a heart that will honour you | 38 |

## Purpose
| | |
|---|---|
| The Tango of our lives | 146 |

## Obedience
| | |
|---|---|
| Called by Christ to be disciples | 13 |
| Christ, my teacher | 16 |
| Give me a heart that will honour you | 38 |

## Repentence and Forgiveness
| | |
|---|---|
| At this day's end | 5 |
| At this table we remember | 6 |
| Forgive us when our deeds ignore | 32 |
| I live, dependent on Jesus | 61 |
| I was lost but now I'm found | 63 |
| In an age of twisted values | 67 |
| O Lord, how long | 112 |
| O Love that searches all my soul | 114 |
| The gracious invitiation | 137 |

## Risk
| | |
|---|---|
| The man of the margins | 141 |

## Salvation
| | |
|---|---|
| From opposite directions | 35 |
| O Lord, you've searched me | 113 |
| Sing the gospel of salvation | 130 |

**Serving**

| | |
|---|---|
| Be the hands of Jesus | 10 |
| Called by Christ to be disciples | 13 |
| Finding a way | 28 |
| God of present, God of past | 45 |
| Good Joseph was a man | 47 |
| Is the church a building? | 72 |
| Lord Jesus, plant a seed of faith | 94 |

**Temptation and trials**

| | |
|---|---|
| Christ, here we are! | 15 |
| The path is stony | 143 |
| The Tango of our lives | 146 |
| There's a long way | 148 |

**Transformed lives**

| | |
|---|---|
| And can we hope | 4 |
| Breathe in me, Lord | 11 |
| Christ, here we are! | 15 |
| For riches of salvation | 30 |
| How amazing | 56 |
| I was lost but now I'm found | 63 |
| Out of the darkness of the night | 121 |

**Truth**

| | |
|---|---|
| Christ, my teacher | 16 |
| God has called us to a journey | 40 |
| In an age of twisted values | 67 |

**Trust**

| | |
|---|---|
| Breathe in me, Lord | 11 |
| I lift my eyes to the hills | 60 |
| Let us rejoice | 85 |
| Lord, you amaze us | 98 |
| Lord, you have blessed me | 99 |
| Set the sail on your boat | 127 |
| This heavenly love brings life | 151 |

# PAIN AND SUFFERING

| | |
|---|---|
| An urgent voice is calling | 3 |
| Cry 'Freedom!' | 21 |
| Draw us together at the close of day | 23 |
| For those who strive for justice | 31 |
| Hear our prayer for others | 54 |
| In the night, the sound of crying | 69 |
| Jesus meets us at the margins | 75 |
| O God of hope | 109 |

| | |
|---|---|
| O West Bank town of Bethlehem | 115 |
| Open our eyes to see | 117 |
| Where love is met with hatred | 165 |

# PEACE

| | |
|---|---|
| At this table we remember | 6 |
| From opposite directions | 35 |
| God of the nations | 46 |
| Hear our prayer for others | 54 |
| In an age of twisted values | 67 |
| It's the morning after | 73 |
| O God of hope | 109 |
| O Lord, how long | 112 |
| The day will come | 136 |
| What can we say? | 162 |

# PROTEST

| | |
|---|---|
| From opposite directions | 35 |
| In an age of twisted values | 67 |
| It's the morning after | 73 |
| Let the world be changed | 83 |
| O Lord, how long | 112 |
| We hear the cry, Lord | 155 |

# SEASONS

**Advent and Christmas**

| | |
|---|---|
| Fearful, uncertain | 26 |
| From a manger in a stable | 33 |
| From the heart of God the Father | 36 |
| From the heights of glory | 37 |
| Hallelu, hallelu, hallelujah | 50 |
| In the night, the sound of crying | 69 |
| Light of her life | 86 |
| Mary, blessèd teenage mother | 100 |
| Mother of Christ, called from above | 102 |
| No gift so wonderful | 103 |
| O West Bank town of Bethlehem | 115 |
| One of us, flesh and blood | 116 |
| People, look east | 122 |
| The promised time arrives | 144 |

**Lent**

| | |
|---|---|
| Christ, here we are! | 15 |
| The gracious invitation | 137 |

**Mothering Sunday**
The Lord created family 139
When we were little, hurt and lost 164

**Palm Sunday, Passiontide**
A crown of piercing thorns 1
From opposite directions 35
From the heights of glory 37
How did you feel, Lord Jesus 57
Lord, what a sacrifice I see 97
Now is the time 106
Room prepared; disciples meet 124
Sing, my tongue, the glorious struggle 129
The only power that cleanses me 142
Together we proclaim 153
What a night to remember 161

**Easter**
From the heights of glory 37
How did you feel, Lord Jesus 57
In the peace of a garden 70
Sad, confused and shaken 125

**Ascentiontide**
Every land in all creation 24
Hallelujah 51

**Pentecost**
The Spirit of God 145

**Harvest**
Lord, at a time when our
    tables are laden 91
We owe our thanks to you, Lord 156

# WORLD
**Creation**
Called by Christ to be disciples 13
Creation sings! 20
We remember you 157

**Power**
From opposite directions 35

**War**
God of the nations 46
O Christ, remember them 107
O God of hope 109

# WORSHIP
**Adoration**
Gracious God, in adoration 49
Let all creation's wonders 80
Our Father (Caribbean) 119

**Blessing**
B-b-b Bless this hard city 8

**Confession**
In an age of twisted values 67
Let us all, with grateful minds 84
Lord, we know that we have failed you 96
O Lord, how long 112
The gracious invitation 137
We've silenced our prophets 160

**Confirmation**
Christ, my teacher 16
Give me a heart that will honour you 38
Let love be our glory 81
Lord Jesus, plant a seed of faith 94

**Evening**
At this day's end 5
Draw us together at the close of day 23
Now as the evening shadows fall 104

**Funeral**
O Father, on your love we call 108

**Holy Communion**
At this table we remember 6
At your feet 7
Now, come to the water 105
Room prepared; disciples meet 124
Tell, my tongue, the awesome
    mystery 135
Thirsty for the living water 150
Together we proclaim 153
What a night to remember 161

**Intercession, Petition**
B-b-b Bless this hard city 8
Christ, my teacher 16
God of love 44
God of the nations 46
Hear our prayer for others 54

| | |
|---|---|
| Is the church a building? | 72 |
| Let love be our glory | 81 |
| Lord, change the world | 92 |
| Lord Jesus, plant a seed of faith | 94 |
| O Christ, remember them | 107 |
| O Lord, how long | 112 |
| Our Father in heaven | 120 |
| The path is stony | 143 |
| We will pray for you, sister | 159 |

## Marriage
| | |
|---|---|
| And can we hope | 4 |
| Let love be our glory | 81 |
| This heavenly love brings | 151 |

## One World Week
| | |
|---|---|
| And can we hope | 4 |
| Every land in all creation | 24 |
| God of the nations | 46 |
| Jesus shall reign | 76 |
| Justice like a river | 79 |
| Let love be our glory | 81 |
| Let the world be changed | 83 |
| Lord, change our world | 92 |
| Now, come to the water | 105 |
| O Lord, how long | 112 |
| The day will come | 136 |
| We will pray for you, sister | 159 |

## Ordination/Commissioning
| | |
|---|---|
| Be the hands of Jesus | 10 |
| Called by Christ to be disciples | 13 |
| Called to shed light | 14 |
| Christ, my teacher | 16 |
| Give me a heart that will honour you | 38 |
| Is the church a building? | 72 |
| Let love be our glory | 81 |
| Lord Jesus, plant a seed of faith | 94 |

## Praise
| | |
|---|---|
| All nations of the world | 2 |
| Bring to God your new, best songs | 12 |
| Come with newly-written anthems | 18 |
| Creating God, we bring our songs of praise | 19 |
| Creation sings! | 20 |
| Every land in all creation | 24 |
| Extol the God of justice | 25 |
| God is our strength | 42 |
| God of life, we come in worship | 43 |
| God of present, God of past | 45 |
| Hallelu, hallelu, hallelujah | 50 |
| Hallelujah | 51 |
| How amazing | 56 |
| Humble yourselves | 59 |
| I lift my eyes to the hills | 60 |
| I stand on a rock | 62 |
| I will always sing the praises | 64 |
| Jesus shall reign | 76 |
| Jesus, the Holy One | 77 |
| Let all creation's wonders | 80 |
| Let us all, with grateful minds | 84 |
| Light of her life | 86 |
| Lord, today your voice is calling | 95 |
| Lord, you amaze us | 98 |
| Lord, you have blessed me | 99 |
| Out of the darkness of the night | 121 |
| Praise to Christ, the Lord incarnate | 123 |
| Sound out his praises | 131 |
| This side of heaven | 152 |
| We owe our thanks to you, Lord | 156 |

## Remembrance
| | |
|---|---|
| God of the nations | 46 |
| In glad and sad remembrance | 68 |
| O Christ, remember them | 107 |
| We remember you | 157 |

## Thanksgiving
| | |
|---|---|
| For beauty which delights our eyes | 29 |
| For riches of salvation | 30 |
| God of life, we come in worship | 43 |
| God of present, God of past | 45 |
| Hallelujah | 51 |
| How amazing | 56 |
| Lord, today your voice is calling | 95 |
| Lord, you amaze us | 98 |
| The only power that cleanses me | 142 |
| We owe our thanks to you, Lord | 156 |

# INDEX OF FIRST LINES AND TITLES

*This index gives the first line of each hymn. If a hymn is known by an alternative title, this is also given, but indented and in italics.*

| | |
|---|---|
| A crown of piercing thorns | 1 |
| All nations of the world | 2 |
| *All the time* | 27 |
| An urgent voice is calling | 3 |
| And can we hope | 4 |
| At this day's end | 5 |
| At this table we remember | 6 |
| At your feet | 7 |
| B-b-b Bless this hard city | 8 |
| Be the God of all my Sundays | 9 |
| Be the hands of Jesus | 10 |
| Breathe in me, Lord | 11 |
| Bring to God your new, best songs | 12 |
| *Broken image* | 158 |
| Called by Christ to be disciples | 13 |
| Called to shed light | 14 |
| Christ, here we are! | 15 |
| Christ, my teacher | 16 |
| Come, rest in the love of Jesus | 17 |
| Come with newly-written anthems | 18 |
| Creating God, we bring our songs of praise | 19 |
| Creation sings! | 20 |
| Cry 'Freedom!' | 21 |
| Don't be afraid | 22 |
| Draw us together at the close of day | 23 |
| Every land in all creation | 24 |
| Extol the God of justice | 25 |
| *Faithful God* | 22 |
| Fearful, uncertain | 26 |
| Feast your mind on what is pure | 27 |
| Finding a way | 28 |
| For beauty which delights our eyes | 29 |
| *For I can do all things* | 61 |
| For riches of salvation | 30 |
| For those who strive for justice | 31 |
| Forgive us when our deeds ignore | 32 |
| From a manger in a stable | 33 |
| From near and far | 34 |
| From opposite directions | 35 |
| From the heart of God the Father | 36 |
| From the heights of glory | 37 |
| Give me a heart that will honour you | 38 |
| *Give thanks* | 30 |
| God beyond earth's finest treasures | 39 |
| God has called us to a journey | 40 |
| God has promised many things | 41 |
| God is our strength from days of old | 42 |
| God of life, we come in worship | 43 |
| God of love | 44 |
| God of present, God of past | 45 |
| God of the nations | 46 |
| *God of the second chance* | 15 |
| *God's surprise* | 128 |
| Good Joseph was a man | 47 |
| Good Lord, deliver us | 48 |
| *Good news to the poor* | 145 |
| Gracious God, in adoration | 49 |
| Hallelu, hallelu, hallelujah | 50 |
| Hallelujah | 51 |
| *Hallelujah Chorus* | 51 |
| Happy to share | 52 |
| *Have we any room for Jesus?* | 103 |
| He broke the rules | 53 |
| Hear our prayer for others | 54 |
| Hold tight | 55 |
| How amazing | 56 |
| How did you feel, Lord Jesus | 57 |

| | |
|---|---|
| How rich and deep God's judgements are | 58 |
| Humble yourselves | 59 |
| I lift my eyes to the hills | 60 |
| I live, dependent on Jesus | 61 |
| I stand on a rock | 62 |
| I was lost but now I'm found | 63 |
| I will always sing the praises | 64 |
| If we have never sought | 65 |
| Image of our God and Father | 66 |
| In an age of twisted values | 67 |
| In glad and sad remembrance | 68 |
| In the night, the sound of crying | 69 |
| In the peace of a garden | 70 |
| In vast, ornate cathedrals | 71 |
| Is the church a building? | 72 |
| It's the morning after | 73 |
| *Jesus came to save us* | *124* |
| Jesus, in your life we see you | 74 |
| Jesus meets us at the margins | 75 |
| *Jesus of the scars* | *65* |
| Jesus shall reign, his power be shown | 76 |
| Jesus, the Holy One | 77 |
| Jesus, we have heard your Spirit | 78 |
| Justice like a river | 79 |
| Let all creation's wonders | 80 |
| *Let justice roll* | *160* |
| Let love be our glory | 81 |
| Let love be real | 82 |
| Let the world be changed | 83 |
| Let us all, with grateful minds | 84 |
| Let us rejoice | 85 |
| Light of her life | 86 |
| Listen up | 87 |
| Living God, your word has called us | 88 |
| Living water | 89 |
| Long ago you taught your people | 90 |
| Lord, at a time when our tables are laden | 91 |
| Lord, change our world | 92 |
| *Lord, close to you* | *143* |
| Lord, give us vision | 93 |
| Lord Jesus, plant a seed of faith | 94 |
| Lord, today your voice is calling | 95 |
| Lord, we know that we have failed you | 96 |
| Lord, what a sacrifice I see | 97 |
| Lord, you amaze us | 98 |
| Lord, you have blessed me | 99 |
| Mary, blessèd teenage mother | 100 |
| Mighty, magnificent God | 101 |
| Mother of Christ, called from above | 102 |
| *Mothers of the world* | *164* |
| No gift so wonderful | 103 |
| Now as the evening shadows fall | 104 |
| Now, come to the water | 105 |
| Now is the time | 106 |
| O Christ, remember them | 107 |
| O Father, on your love we call | 108 |
| O God of hope | 109 |
| O God of thoughts and feelings | 110 |
| O holy, heavenly kingdom | 111 |
| O Lord, how long | 112 |
| O Lord, you've searched me | 113 |
| O Love that searches all my soul | 114 |
| O West Bank town of Bethlehem | 115 |
| *Oh, what a day!* | *152* |
| One of us, flesh and blood | 116 |
| Open our eyes to see | 117 |
| Open the door | 118 |
| Our Father (Caribbean) | 119 |
| Our Father in heaven | 120 |
| Out of the darkness of the night | 121 |
| People, look east | 122 |
| Praise to Christ, the Lord incarnate | 123 |
| Room prepared; disciples meet | 124 |
| Sad, confused and shaken | 125 |
| Saviour, precious Saviour | 126 |
| Set the sail on your boat | 127 |
| Sing 'Hey!' for the God who is eternally new | 128 |
| Sing, my tongue, the glorious struggle | 129 |
| Sing the gospel of salvation | 130 |
| Sound out his praises | 131 |

| | | | |
|---|---|---|---|
| Such a host as none can number | 132 | This side of heaven | 152 |
| Teach me, dear Lord | 133 | Together we proclaim | 153 |
| Teach us how to walk | 134 | We have a vision | 154 |
| Tell, my tongue, the awesome mystery | 135 | We hear your cry, Lord | 155 |
| | | We owe our thanks to you, Lord | 156 |
| *That's why we're here* | 52 | We remember you | 157 |
| The day will come, that glorious day | 136 | We saw beauty in the ashes | 158 |
| The gracious invitation | 137 | We will pray for you, sister | 159 |
| *The greatest love* | 97 | We've silenced our prophets | 160 |
| The heavens proclaim God's glory | 138 | *What a gift* | 37 |
| The Lord created family | 139 | What a night to remember | 161 |
| The Lord reveals his glory | 140 | What can we say? | 162 |
| The man of the margins | 141 | When the day grows cold | 163 |
| The only power that cleanses me | 142 | When we were little, hurt and lost | 164 |
| The path is stony | 143 | Where love is met with hatred | 165 |
| The promised time arrives | 144 | *Where you lead us* | 78 |
| The Spirit of God | 145 | Where you're going I will follow | 166 |
| The Tango of our lives | 146 | Within the busy rush of life | 167 |
| The universe was waiting | 147 | *Wonderful, glorious day!* | 121 |
| There's a long way | 148 | You are the Bread of Life | 168 |
| There's a time come nearer | 149 | You've called us as your Church, Lord | 169 |
| Thirsty for the living water | 150 | | |
| This heavenly love brings life | 151 | | |